California Criminal Law Workbook

Ninth Edition

W. Douglas Haynes

Professor, Administration of Justice Department
Cerritos College, Norwalk, California

When used in conjunction with related classroom lecture, this workbook satisfies the minimum standards established by the California Community Colleges Chancellor's Office and the California Peace Officer Standards and training Commission for the two courses "Concepts of Criminal Law" and California Substantive Criminal Law" (or "Criminal Law I" and "Criminal Law II")

Kendall Hunt
publishing company

Legal Workbook Series

California Criminal Procedure Workbook
  W. Douglas Haynes, 1974, 1977, 1990, 1994

Legal Research
  Richard F. McGrath, 1972, 1973, 1976

California Criminal Evidence
  Marvin Engquist, 1989, 1994

Kendall Hunt
publishing company

www.kendallhunt.com
Send all inquiries to:
4050 Westmark Drive
Dubuque, IA 52004-1840

ISBN 978-1-5249-0305-3

Printed in the United States of America

Contents

Preface

This workbook is designed to provide a simple note taking aid for students enrolled in college or police academy criminal law classes.

It should be used in the classroom and for outside study and review in an organized course with a qualified instructor. It is not intended to be used for individual self-study, although it could be beneficial for such use by helping a student to organize his or her reading and study methods.

The workbook utilizes several unique features:

- *Note taking Outline:* The note-taking outline is the most important feature of the workbook. It is used in class in place of the usual note taking materials. It eases the task of reducing the instructor's lecture to written notes by providing an organized framework of the lecture to be filled-in with short, pertinent notes during classroom lectures. This organizes and simplifies the note taking process, while still requiring the student to be attentive to the instructor's lecture.

- *Self-Instruction Programs:* Unique programmed lessons are used for self-instruction outside of class. They use the same principles as employed in computerized teaching programs. Three chapters of the workbook are presented in this manner and provide a refreshing departure from routine reading assignments.

- *Problem Exercises:* Exercises are included in each chapter. They consist of true-false, fill-in and short essay questions to be completed as homework assignments or in classroom group study. The essay problems provide interesting practical situations to test a student's ability to apply the law to real live situations.

- *Study Aids:* A number of charts, diagrams and check lists provide a variety of tools to help the student in learning complex legal material.

- *Discussion Guides:* Discussion guides are provided to organize and facilitate group discussions of the major concepts presented in class.

Note to instructors:

An instructor's manual is available which may be ordered directly from the author. The manual includes:

- Complete lesson plans and lecture outlines for each chapter of the student workbook. The lecture outlines are arranged in well spaced, easy to follow outline format, ready to be used as classroom lecture notes by anyone with just a minimum of subject matter preparation.

- Teaching suggestions for organizing group discussions, student assignments and classroom activities.

- One manual is provided free of charge to instructors adopting the workbook for required classroom use. Additional copies are available at $300.00 each.

The following materials are also available to registered instructors:

- Complete answer keys for all problems and exercises in the student workbook.

- Sample copies of handouts, study guides and other classroom materials which may be duplicated for student use.

- A computer data bank of exam questions organized by workbook chapters.

Address all inquiries to:
Professor W. Douglas Haynes
Cerritos College
Administration of Justice Department
11110 Alondra Bl.
Norwalk, CA 90650 – 6298
562.860.2451 Ext. 2779
Fax: 562.467.5005

Part I

Concepts of Criminal Law

Part I of this workbook is an introduction to the general concepts of criminal law, including the different types of laws, California sentencing laws, probation, parole, corpus Delicti, elements of crimes, act and intent, parties to a crime, defenses to crimes, and Constitutional Law. It provides an overview of the general theories, concepts and principles of California criminal law. It does not examine the definitions and description of individual crimes. A detailed analysis of the statutes and case decisions describing all common California crimes is provided in Part II of the workbook.

Par I satisfies all of the requirement of the California Peace Officers Standards and Training Commission's Regular Basic Course for the following Learning Domain:
#5 – Introduction to Criminal Law:

This part of the workbook also examines components of the following Learning Domains. They are not part of the required P.O.S.T. content for the Concepts of Criminal Law class and may duplicate material from other classes, but they are still worthwhile to include considering the educational value of repetition and review.
#2 – Criminal Justice System
#15 – Laws of Arrest
#17 – Presentation of Evidence
#20 – Use of Force

This part of the workbook also satisfies all of the requirements of the old P.O.S.T. Learning Domain #14 – Constitutional Law, which has been deleted from the Basic Course and included in a reduced format in Learning Domain #2.

Chapter 1

Introduction to Law

Introduction

This first chapter will acquaint you with the major categories and forms of law provide you with a brief history of law and introduce several important concepts of criminal law. It also provides opportunities for class discussions about the role of criminal law and law enforcement in society.

The chapter consists of five parts:

1. A programmed lesson describing the history and development of criminal law, used as a self-paced, self - directed learning program, for independent study outside of class.
2. A note-taking outline of the class lectures, describing the different kinds of laws and how they affect society. The outline directly conforms to the instructor's lecture and is used to take notes during class lectures. It is all you will nee to take notes in class. No other note taking materials are necessary.
3. Supplemental reading material on interpreting court report case citations.
4. Class discussion questions concerning criminal justice policies, concepts and procedures.
5. Several self-help activities, including problem solving exercises, true-false questions, vocabulary definitions and exercises in the use of the Penal Code.

Objectives

When you complete this chapter, including the classroom lectures, the related reading and workbook assignment and the recommended class activities you should be able to do the following (Note: the numbers in parentheses refer to P.O.S.T. Commission learning domains):

1. Identify the Code of Hammurabi and the Code of Justinian as two of the earliest sources of written law.
2. List the forms of early English law and the types of courts established by William the First of England and explain how they led to the development of the English common law and modern American law. (LD5-3.1.6)
3. Describe and be able to distinguish between statute law, case law, civil law, criminal law, substantive law and procedural law. Explain the significance of each in relation to modern law enforcement. (LD5-3.1.6)
4. Describe how case law interprets statute law.
5. Define the term "Stare Decisis". (LD5-3.1.6)
6. Describe the importance of procedural law in criminal defense.
7. Explain the relationship between the creation of law and its interpretation and enforcement, including the application of enforcement policies based on the "Spirit of the Law" as opposed to the "Letter of the Law". (LD5-3.1.1, 3.1.6)

8. Explain the concept of the balance between loss of freedom and protection from crime in the criminal justice system.

9. Explain the concepts of selective enforcement and discretionary judgment.

10. Describe the decision-making process used by police administrators and individual officers in establishing enforcement policies.

11. Recognize, define, and evaluate your personal attitudes and beliefs about criminal justice and be able to justify your belief with factual evidence and sound reasoning.

12. Use the Index and Table of Contents of the California Penal Code to find common criminal statutes and be able to interpret and explain a simple court report case citation.

HISTORY OF LAW
A Programmed Lesson for Self-Instruction
Introduction

This programmed lesson is probably different from the kinds of instruction you have experienced before. It uses the same basic principles that are found in very expensive and complicated computer programs.

Programmed teaching is a type of self-instruction that presents information in small, step-by-step segments. You are periodically tested on what you have learned and directed to review segments that you do not understand. This process of testing and review enables you to learn the information faster and remember it longer than you would by simply reading a conventional textbook.

Instructions

1. On each page of this program you will find a series of numbered paragraphs. As you proceed through the program you will be guided by the instruction at the end of each paragraph.
2. Follow the directions at the end of the paragraph. You usually will be asked a question and given a choice of answers. Select you answer and turn to the paragraph indicated. If you are correct you will be directed to a new material to read. If you are incorrect you will be instructed to turn back to an earlier paragraph for additional study.
3. Continue n this manner, following each instruction and answering all the questions until you have read the entire program.
4. Note that you *do not* read through this programmed lesson page by page. You will do considerable skipping from one page to another, forward and back. Follow the instructions carefully!

Start Here

1. Law is a fascinating subject it encompasses the entire real of human activity. It serves to protect and also to punish. It must provide rigid and unyielding controls against those who would threaten our safety, yet be sufficiently flexible to show compassion to those who unwittingly violate its provisions. It must provide constant standards of conduct based on tradition and the accumulated knowledge of past experience, but it must also be capable of change and growth in a modern society.

   As a police officer, knowledge of the law is the most important tool of your profession. You must learn the law beyond mere memorization of its provisions. You must *understand* the law so that you can apply it to living situations.

   Turn to paragraph 9 on the next page.

2. True or False?

   An important objective of this first chapter is to be able to identify the various kinds of laws and recognize the differences between them.

   If this is true, turn to paragraph 13.   NOTE: Don't forget to circle the
   If this is false, turn to paragraph 10.   correct answer on the answer sheet.

---

3. According to our definition, laws are simply those customs and beliefs which we consider sufficiently important to:

   1. Have a definite impact on our lives.
   2. Be believed and adhered to by a majority of the people.
   3. Require obedience through some enforcement authority.

      If 1 is correct, turn to paragraph 14.
      If 2 is correct, turn to paragraph 17.
      If 3 is correct, turn to paragraph 6.

---

4. Right. Legal knowledge is not only desirable; it is essential for success in law enforcement. More than half of all the required courses for a college criminal justice degree are in various aspects of criminal law.

   Go on to paragraph 5.

---

5. In this first chapter, you will learn some definitions of the word "law" and some of the history of law. We will also devote some class time to discussion of the reasons why laws are necessary in our society and what purposes they serve. Finally, you will learn how our laws are created and, most importantly, the various kinds of laws and how they differ.

   Turn to paragraph 2.

---

6. Right. This is the primary feature that distinguishes laws from customs. In the case of law obedience is enforced while strict obedience is not required in the case of customs and courtesies.

   Continue to paragraph 7.

---

7. True or False?

   As a police officer you will be called upon to enforce customs as well as laws.

      If this is true, turn to paragraph 24.
      If this is false, turn to paragraph 21.

---

8. True or False?

   The creation of rules of conduct is a relatively recent concept in the history of man.

   If this is true, turn to paragraph 19.
   If this is false, turn to paragraph 16.

9. True or False?

   A study of law is desirable, but not essential, to a successful police officer. It is less important than a knowledge of fingerprints, firearms or radio operations for example.

   If the above statement is true, turn to   Note: Circle your answer on the
   paragraph 12.   answer sheet at the end of this
   If the above statement is false, turn to   programmed lesson, before turning to
   paragraph 4.   paragraph 12 or 4.

10. Sorry, that's exactly what we're going to do. Quite a bit of time will be spent on learning about the various kinds of laws and how each type differs from the others. For example, a police officer must be able to recognize the differences between what is called "civil" law and "criminal" law so that s/he will know when a matter requires action by the police and when it is something to be handled by the parties involved and their attorneys and insurance companies.

   Reread paragraph 5 and continue from there.

11. Now let's look at the definition of the word "law." First, the Anglo-Saxon (early English) meaning of the word was simply: "that which is established." In other words, it is something that exists or has been created by some higher authority. The dictionary defines many forms of established law: natural law, Church law, mathematical laws, the laws of physics, gravity, etc.

   A more specific definition that can be applied to the type of law, which we are studying, would be the following:

   "Laws are those customs and beliefs of any group of people which are considered sufficiently important to have obedience enforced by some authority."

   Laws supposedly reflect the traditions, beliefs and way of life of a majority of the people in a community. Some customs are too minor to be made into laws. Certain traditions and courtesies, although desirable, are not considered sufficiently important to require adherence by everyone and therefore are not enforced as laws.

   Under a democratic system, the law is an expression of the beliefs of a majority of the people and should reflect their important social customs.

   Turn to paragraph 3.

12. No, you're wrong. A knowledge of law is the most important skill of the successful police officer. It is the skill that he or she uses most frequently. Without an understanding of law, their other abilities have little value.

   Turn to paragraph 5.

13. Good. You're correct. We will learn quite a bit about the various forms of law and go into some detail in studying their differences.

   You seem to be getting the hang of this

   Go on to paragraph 11.

14. Laws have a definite impact on our lives, but so do most customs and traditions, whether they are made into laws or not. Answer 1 is not quite correct. The more important distinction is that obedience is required in the case of laws by not in the case of simple customs. We can be punished for violating a law but not for a violation of courteous behavior.

Continue on to paragraph 15.

15. True or False?

As a police officer, you will be called upon to enforce customs as well as laws.

If this is true, turn to paragraph 26.
If this is false, turn to paragraph 21.

16. That's right. Some form of regulation has always existed. Initially, it was very crude and consisted of only the barest rules necessary for survival. Gradually, as society became more complex, a greater number of regulations were required in order for men to live in harmony with one another. Unfortunately, we have a tendency today to look upon the law as a panacea, capable of curing all our ills. Whenever we find something undesirable in our society, we pass a law in an effort to correct it. Eventually, we must realize that laws cannot accomplish all things and that although the law can punish a dishonest man, it cannot change him into an honest one.

Turn to paragraph 25.

17. Yes, laws are believed and adhered to by a majority of the people. But so are customs, whether they are made into laws or not. The more important distinction is that obedience is required in the case of laws but not in the case of simple customs. We can be punished for violating a law but not for violation of courteous behavior.

Answer 2 was not quite correct, for question paragraph number 3. The correct answer was number 3.

Continue on to paragraph 18.

18. True or False?

As a police officer you will be called upon to enforce customs as well as laws.

If this is true, turn to paragraph 26.
If this is false, turn to paragraph 21.

19. No, that's not true. We have had some form of law since the earliest history of man. When primitive cave dwellers first gathered food and then fought others to maintain its possession, they were practicing a most basic legal concept: ownership and the right to defend one's property.

This simple idea gradually evolved into more sophisticated rules of conduct, but out activities have had some form of regulation from the very beginning of civilization.
Return to paragraph 8, answer the question correctly, and then continue on from there.

20. Which of the following statements is true?

    1. Much of our law today originated as religious beliefs.
    2. Our law does not reflect religious beliefs because of the constitutional provision for the separation of church and state.
    3. If a state law and a church rule are in conflict, the church rule will prevail because it is based on higher authority.

    If 1 is true, turn to paragraph 23.
    If 2 is true, turn to paragraph 27.
    If 3 is true, turn to paragraph 29.

21. Correct. There will be many times when you will see the customs and traditions of common decency violated. People will be discourteous and arrogant to each other and to you. They may deliberately turn their backs on those in need. But always remember: you have authority to enforce the law, but you cannot attempt to enforce good manners. Unless a breach of common courtesies becomes a violation of law, you have no authority to take action against the offending party

    Proceed on to paragraph 22.

22. Let's continue on and discuss some of the early history of laws.

    The earliest laws were simply those rules of conduct recognized by the family and enforced by the head of the household. This is still the basis of law in some primitive societies. As social units became larger and expanded into clans, tribes, and villages, the concept of law expanded with them. Each tribe developed its own rules based on concepts that were agreeable to all members. These rules were created and enforced by the tribal elders. Frequently, enforcement was based on group responsibility, with an entire family or village being punished for the transgressions of one member.

    Turn to paragraph 8.

23. Number 1 was correct. A good part of our law today was originally based 9on religious beliefs. Among these are the laws concerning murder, assault, rape, theft, divorce, marriage and many others.

    Turn to paragraph 30.

24. No, this is not true. There will be many times when you will see the customs and traditions of common decency violated. People will be discourteous and arrogant to each other and to you. They may deliberately turn their backs on those in desperate need. But always remember: you have the authority to enforce the law, but you cannot attempt to enforce good manners. Unless a breach of common courtesy goes far enough to become a violation of law, you have no authority to take action against the offending party.

    Turn to paragraph 22.

25. As society became more complex, the law grew in complexity also. Eventually its creation and administration were given over to people who were specially trained for the task. Frequently, the early laws were based on religious beliefs and were established and enforced by the priesthood. Our laws today still reflect much of the Judeo-Christian religious ethic.

Some medieval religious order devoted their entire live to painstakingly transcribing Papal and royal edicts into written form. Many laws and customs were simply passed on through generations of tribesmen by word of mouth.

In approximately 1760 B.C. what is believed to be the first written code of laws was issued. Hammurabi, King of Babylon, compiled all of the laws of his country onto one tablet consisting of 28 sections. Prior to this, a person seeking to know the law would be required to search through many individual documents and listen to the teaching of many different men to gain this knowledge. Now, all the law was readily available in one work, the Code of Hammurabi. Today, we recognize this stone tablet as the first written code of laws.

A similar early law book, called the Akkadian Code of Eshnuna, has been uncovered in Iraq. It is possible that it may predate the Code of Hammurabi, but until further proof is presented, Hammurabi' Code is still considered the first code of law.

Another historic legal treatise was the Code of Justinian, written in Rome in 535 A.D. The early Romans were so noted for their legal system that they were often referred to as "the law givers." The Code of Justinian, also known as the Corpus Juris Civilis, had a great effect on the formation of English law, and through England, on American law of today.

Turn to paragraph 20.

26. No, this is not true. There will be many time when you will see the customs and traditions of common decency violated. People will be discourteous and arrogant to each other and to you. They may deliberately turn their backs on those in desperate need. But always remember: you have the authority to enforce the law, but you cannot attempt to enforce good manners. Unless a breach of common courtesy goes far enough to become a violation of law, you have no authority to take action against the offending party.

You have just missed two questions in a row.
Go back to paragraph 11 and reread from that point on.

27. Nope, sorry. Although the state cannot interfere with the operation of a church and vice versa, many of our laws originated as church edicts. Among these are the laws concerning murder, assault, rape, theft, divorce, marriage and many others. Number 1 was correct.

Go to paragraph 30.

28. Here are the correct answers:

    1. Corpus Juris Civilis was also known as the Code of Justinian
    2. Hammurabi was King of Babylon.
    3. Code of Hammurabi was written in 1760 B.C. (give or take a hundred years or so)
    4. Code of Justinian was written in 535 A.D.
    5. First written code of laws was the Code of Hammurabi.

Go on to paragraph 31.

29. Even though the church rule may be based on pretty high authority, the state law would still prevail as long as it did not unconstitutionally interfere with the operation of the church. An example of this would be the state law that permits first cousins to marry, even though this is contrary to the edicts of some churches. In this case the state law precedence over the church law.

Turn to paragraph 23.

---

30. Fill in the correct words and phrases below and on the answer sheet.

1. The Corpus Juris Civilis was also known as _____
2. Hammurabi was the King of _____
3. The Cod of Hammurabi was written in _____ (year)
4. The Code of Justinian was written in _____(year)
5. The first recognized written code of laws was the Code of_____

Turn to paragraph 28.

---

31. As our final step in this very brief study of the history of law we'll explore the development of the English legal system. The law of England was the forerunner of American law and still influences our legal concepts today.

The history of English law starts with the beginning of English national government in 1066 A.D. In that year, William the Conqueror invaded Anglo-Saxon England from Normandy (France), united the many separate leaders, and established himself as King. One of his first acts was to establish a judicial system consisting of three levels of courts.

The lowest court was known as the Baronial Court and was presided over by the local landowners. Its law was called Baronial Law. Next, the King's Court, administered by the King himself, resolved disputes between noblemen and created the King's Law. The common man could not seek a hearing in the King's Court. The third court was the Ecclesiastical or Church Court in which disputes involving the many activities of life controlled by church law were decided. Its law was known as Ecclesiastical or Canon Law.

Let's see what you've learned so far about the start of the English legal system.

Please turn to paragraph 35.

---

32. The authority of the Baronial court was severely abused by many of the minor noblemen who administered this court. Decisions frequently favored the wealthy landowners with little regard for the welfare of the commoners. Some of their ideas of justice were crude and there was little uniformity in the decision rendered by different courts. Every Baronial Court was independent so that armed conflict frequently resulted when the opinions of two adjacent courts differed.

Because of these deficiencies in the Baronial Courts, they were eventually abolished and the King's Law was extended to everyone through a system of circuit courts with traveling judges appointed by the King.

(continue on to the next page)

As these judges traveled throughout the kingdom, their decisions and opinions were permanently recorded and a uniform system of law was developed throughout England. This system consisted of the accumulated opinions given in the thousands of case decisions rendered by these judges. This vast body of legal knowledge eventually became known as the "common law" of England and is the foundation of most of our legal principles in America.

Turn to paragraph 42.

33. The correct answers are list below:

    1. Baronial Courts
    2. King's Court
    3. Ecclesiastical Courts

(Not necessarily in the above order.)

       Did you get them all right?
       Was your spelling correct?
       Please turn to paragraph 39.

34. Sorry, turn to paragraph 37.

35. There were three separate types of courts established by William I.

List the names of these three courts below and on the answer sheet.

    1. _____

    2. _____

    3. _____

When you have completed the above, please turn to paragraph 33.

36. Sorry, go to paragraph 37.

37. Number 3 was right! Titled noblemen were the only segment of the population permitted to be heard in the King's Court. A commoner had no voice here whatever and could gain access only to the less desirable Baronial Court. This was one of the failings of the early English court system, which led to the changes that we will now discuss.   Go to paragraph 32.

38. Sorry, go to paragraph 37.

39. Under William I of England, the King's Court was originally available to only what segment of the population?
    1. Everyone.   Circle the correct answer here and follow the
    2. The King only.   Instructions below.
    3. Titled noblemen only.
    4. Church leaders only.
    5. Merchants only.

(continue on to the next page)

If your answer is 1 turn to paragraph 34.
If your answer is 2 turn to paragraph 36.
If your answer is 3 turn to paragraph 37.
If your answer is 4 turn to paragraph 38.
If your answer is 5 turn to paragraph 41.

40. If your answer to paragraph 42 was 1, 2 or 3 you missed it.

Go back and reread paragraph 32 until you agree that answer number 4 is right.

When you have completed that, you have reached the end of the program. Continue on to the next page to learn how to use this programmed lesson as a review for exam preparation and also to test how much you've learned from the program.

41. Sorry, turn to paragraph 37.

42. The common law of England is based on: (circle the correct answer)

1. Laws passed by parliament.
2. Laws created by the King.
3. Laws passed by local barons.
4. Laws created by the decisions of judges

Turn to paragraph 40.

Program Study Notes

For study purposes, the paragraphs in this programmed lesson may be read in the following order:

1
5
11
21
22
16
25
31
32

Following this order will eliminate those paragraphs, which merely provide instructions and questions and will permit you to proceed through the lesson by reading only the paragraphs containing factual information.

Do not use this outline for your initial study of the lesson. It's important that you follow all of the directions the first time through in order to achieve the full benefit from the programmed learning methods.

Remember, don't use this outline except as a study guide for review after you have completed the program as directed.

Test Yourself

To be certain you understand the material you have just completed, answer the following questions about the history and definition of law. The numbers in parentheses are the paragraph numbers where the answer may be found.

1. Define Ecclesiastical Law: (31)

2. What is the main difference between customs and laws? (11, 3, 6)

3. How long have laws existed? (22, 8, 16, 19)

4. What was the first written code of laws? (25)

5. Most American law is founded upon an earlier from of law. What is that earlier law? (32)

TYPES OF LAWS AND THEIR CHARACTERISTICS

Lecture Notes Outline (To be used during class lectures.)

I.   Types of law:

    A.   Classifications:

        1. _____ and _____ .

        2. _____ and _____ .

        3. _____ and _____ .

Statute Law	Case Law
A. Created by:	Created by:
1. Duality of law:	
2. Pre-emption:	
B. Compiled in:	Compiled in:
C. Purpose and effect:	Purpose and effect:
Example of statute law (459 PC)	Example of case law (Peo. Vs. Miller):

D. Stare Decisis (case law only):

    1.

    2

E. Common Law:

    1. Definition:

    2. Origin of American Law:

      a. Exception:

    3. American Common Law:

      a. "Code" States:

      b. "Common Law" States:

III. Civil Law and Criminal Law:

Civil Law	Criminal Law
A. Definition:	Definition: (683 PC)
B. Plaintiff:	Plaintiff: (684-685 PC) Refusal to prosecute:
C. Title of Action:	Title of Action:
D. Objectives:	Objectives:

Civil Law	Criminal Law
Objectives: (cont'd)	Objectives: (cont'd)
E. Disposition of money collected from defendant:	Disposition of money collected from defendant:
F. Settlement without trial:	Settlement without trial: Plea Bargain:

Civil Law	Criminal Law
G. Imprisonment as an outcome:	Imprisonment as an outcome:

H. Dual liability: (civil and criminal):

IV.   Comparison: Substantive Law and Procedural Law:

Substantive Law	Procedural Law
	Importance:

V.   Purpose and Function of Criminal Law:
   A.   What is law?

   B.   What purpose does law and law enforcement serve?
        1. In a totalitarian society?

        2. In a democratic society?

   C. How does the law protect society?

D.   The dilemma of criminal justice: Freedom vs. protection – the great balancing act.

E.   Goal of the Criminal Law:

F.   How does the law achieve its goals?
   1.   Force vs. Reason:

   2.   Credibility of the law:

G. Enforcement of the law:
   1.   What is law?

   2.   Value of enforcement:

      Charles, Reith, English author and historian: "The finest law written by parliament has no value unless there is _____.

   3.   Foundation of Legal Authority:

1-18

VI. Criminal Justice Discretion:

    A.   Must a peace officer agree with all the laws?

          1.   Objective enforcement of the law:

    B.   Are the police required to take enforcement action against all violators of the law?
          1.   "Letter of the Law":

          2.   "Spirit of the Law":

          3.   "Legislative Intent":

          4.   Officer Discretion:

    C.   Peace Officer Characteristics:
          1.   The "Ideal" Cop:

          2.   The Reality:

          3.   The Perception:

          4.   The Police Kinship:

Case Citations

As discussed in class, case law is compiled in books known as court reports. The location of a particular case can be found in a court report by using an abbreviated identification known as a case citation.

The following is an example of a case citation:

People vs. Wood, 56 Cal. App. 431.

This citation is read in the following manner:

People vs. Wood – Names of the parties. Use of the word "People" indicates that is a criminal case, as all the people of the state are the plaintiffs in a criminal suit. In a civil case the names of the individual parties would appear: (Smith vs. Jones).

Wood is the defendant.

Cal. App. – Refers to the particular series of reports; in this case the California Appellate Reports. These are the cases of the California Court of Appeals.

Cases of the California Supreme Court are reported in the California Reports (abbreviated Cal. Or C)

Another law book series, containing cases from both the California Supreme Court and the Courts of Appeal, is the California Reporter, abbreviated CR

56 – The first number refers to the volume of the particular report series.

431 – The second number refers to the page where the particular case will be found.

Therefore, the written report of the court decision in the criminal case against Wood can be found on page 431 of Volume 56 of the California Appellate Reports.

Reading Assignment

1. Penal Code Section: 1 – 7, 9 – 11, 683 – 685.

Definitions

Define or explain the following:

1. statute law:

2. codes:

3. case law:

4. court reports:

5. stare decisis:

6. appellate court:

7. civil law:

8. plea bargaining:

9. criminal law:

10. common law:

11. deterrent:

12. substantive law:

13. general damages:

14. procedural law:

15. code state:

16. plaintiff:

Penal Code Problems (Record answers here and on your answer sheet)

A Penal Code is a basic legal reference for peace officers. The following problems will introduce you to its use. First examine the Table of Contents and Index in a California Penal Code and then use it to find the answers to the following question. Give Penal code section numbers for each answer.

1. When did the California Penal Code take effect?

2. Define the word "willfully" as used in the Penal Code:

3. Define the word "malice" as used in the Penal Code:

4. When was the last amendment made to section 7 of the Penal Code?

5. Section 4 of the Penal Code declares that its provisions are not necessarily to be strictly construed but rather are to be viewed so as to promote justice. What sections of what other codes are shown as references from this section? (List 3.)

   a. _____ b. _____ c. _____

6. What section of the California Penal Code prohibits the selling of tobacco to minors?

7. What California law prohibits the use of silicone for breast enlargement?

8. Is it lawful to install a two way mirror in a public school restroom? What section of the Penal Code applies to this?

9. You are investigating a kidnapping. A person who has no connection with the kidnapping calls the relatives of the victim and poses as the kidnapper in order to collect the ransom money. What California Penal Code section has he violated?

10. A section of the Penal code permits a prisoner of a county jail or road camp to make blood donations while in jail. What section authorizes this?

True or False:

1. In a civil case the plaintiff is usually the injured victim.

2. In a criminal case the plaintiff is usually the injured victim.

3. A good police investigator must be thoroughly familiar with statute law but needs to know little, if any, case law.

4. Statute law provides the basic framework of the law while case law provides interpretation and applies the statutes to specific situations.

5. If a victim in a criminal case refuses to prosecute, the suspect must be released.

6. Most criminal cases are settled without going to trial.

7. Most civil cases are settled without going to trial.

8. A portion of a fine is usually used to reimburse the victim.

9. Punishment of the defendant is not considered to be a proper objective of the criminal justice system.

10. Procedural law is relatively unimportant for a police officer to know as it applies primarily to civil law rather than criminal law.

Answer here:

	T	F
1.	____	____
2.	____	____
3.	____	____
4.	____	____
5.	____	____
6.	____	____
7.	____	____
8.	____	____
9.	____	____
10.	____	____

Chapter 2

Crime Classifications and Sentencing Laws

Introduction

Chapter One explored the origin and history of law, the various forms and classifications of the law and some major concepts of justice, as it exists today. One method of classifying the law is by dividing it into the two major groupings of civil law and criminal law.

In this chapter we will begin a more detailed examination of that branch of law known as "criminal law." We will particularly study the different classifications of crimes, the types of punishments prescribed and the sentencing laws of California.

Objectives

When you complete this chapter, you should be able to:
1. Explain the legal definition of "crime."
2. Define and distinguish between the classifications of crime known as felonies, misdemeanors, infractions and alternate crimes.
3. Explain the California determinate sentence law including sentence enhancements, consecutive and concurrent sentences, parole, probation and the practice of plea-bargaining.

Lecture Notes Outline

I.   Definition of "crime" (15 PC):

    A.   "Crime" and "public offense":

    B.   Act and failure to act:

C. Punishments:

    1.

    2.

    3.

    4.

    5.

D. Statutory Crimes vs. Common Law Crimes:

E. Ex Post Facto Laws:

II. Classifications of crimes (16, 17 and 1042.5 PC)

A. Distinction between jails and prisons:
    1. Jail:

    2. Prison:

B. Crime Classifications:
    1. Felonies:

    2. Misdemeanors:

    3. Optional or alternate crimes:

4. Infractions (19c, 19d PC):

    a. penalty:

    b. trial:

    c. attorney:

    d. arrest:

III. Penalties:

A. Sentencing Laws (667.5 – 669, 1170 – 1170.16, 2930 – 2932, 12022 – 1022.7 PC):

1. Indeterminate sentencing:

2. Determinate sentencing (117 – 1170.95 PC):

B. Examples of Felony Sentences:

Crime	Sentence
2nd degree burglary, grand theft, forgery, simple assault or battery on a police officer, felony sentence on most optional crimes such as motor vehicle manslaughter, etc.	_____ , _____ or _____
Robbery	_____ , _____ or _____
1st Degree Burglary	_____ , _____ or _____
Manslaughter *(Voluntary)*	_____ , _____ or _____

Forcible rape, simple kidnapping   _____ , _____ or _____

Second-degree murder   _____

First-degree murder, kidnapping for robbery
or ransom   _____

Kidnapping for ransom with injury to the victim,   _____
first-degree murder through us of torture   without possibility of parole.

First-degree murder under certain specified
conditions.   _____

C. Sentence selection (1170(2)(b)PC):

1. Specifically recognized aggravation conditions:

a. Robbery of _____(1170.7 PC).

b. Felony committed because of victim's_____ (1170.75 PC).

c. Robbery or ADW in _____ (1170.8 PC).

d. Arson of _____ (1170.8 PC).

e. Assaulting a _____ (1170.85 PC).

f. Use of obscene matter in child molesting (1170.71 PC).

g. Vulnerability of victim because of _____ (1170.85 PC).

D. Penalty enhancements:

a. Prior convictions (667.5 PC):

(1) Non-violent felonies (667.5(b) PC):

If the defendant is convicted of a non-violent felony and has had any prior felony

conviction within the past _____ years:

an additional _____ may be added to the base penalty for each prior conviction.

(a) Maximum (1170.1a(f) PC):

The maximum total sentence based on enhancements for non-violent prior

convictions is _____ the _____ base sentence.

(2) Serious felonies (667.5a PC):

If a defendant is convicted of a violent felony specified in 667.5c PC and the defendant

has had a similar conviction within the previous _____ years:

an additional _____ years may be added to the base penalty for each prior conviction.

(3) Enhancements for Prior violent Crimes Against Certain Victims (667.9 & 667.10 PC):

(4) Habitual Criminal Laws:

Read the supplemental material at the end of the chapter.

b. Weapons:
    (1) _____ with a _____ (12022 PC):
        (a) meaning of "armed":

        (b) additional penalty:

        (c) liability of co-defendants:

    (2) _____ of a _____ (12022.5 PC):
        (a) meaning of "use":

        (b) additional penalty:

        (c) liability of co-defendants:

    (3) _____ of _____ (12022 PC):
        (a) weapons included:

        (b) additional penalty:

        (c) liability of co-defendants:

    (4) Theory of weapons enhancements:

c. Causing _____ _____ to the victim (12022.7 PC):

    (1) additional penalty:

    (2) liability of co-defendants:

d. Value of stolen or damaged property (12022.6 PC):
    (1) Over $65,000:

    (2) Over $200,000:

    (3) Over $1,300.000:

    (4) Over $3,200,000:

e. Striking the enhancement factors:

f. Dual use of facts:

E. Concurrent and consecutive sentences (669 and 1170.1a PC):

  a. Definitions:
    (1) Concurrent sentence:

    (2) Consecutive sentence:

  b. Maximum consecutive sentences:
    (1) The sentence for each additional crime will be _____ of the _____ sentence for that crime. Enhancement factors cannot be added except for the violent felonies listed in 667.5 PC.

    (2) Regardless of the number of charges, the maximum prison term for any series of non-

    violent felonies is _____ for the total number of consecutive sentences (1170.1a(f) PC)

F. Felony Sentence Calculations:

G. Misdemeanor sentences:

   1. Statute establishes _____sentence.

   2. _____ determines the exact sentence.

   3. Maximum misdemeanor sentence (19a PC):

IV. Parole (2931, 3000 – 3065 PC):

   A. Definition:

   B. Eligibility (3000(a), 3046PC):
      1. Normal:

      2. Life sentences:

         a. Straight Life:

         b. Term to Life:

      3. Loss of Parole Date Credit (2931 – 2932 PC):

         a. Procedure for loss of credit:
            (1) Written Notice:

            (2) Hearing:

      4. Criminal Prosecution (653.76 PC):

C. Length of parole (3000 PC):
   1. Normal (3000 (a) & 3001(a) PC):

   2. Life Sentences (3000(b) & 3000.1(a) PC):
      a. Straight Life:

      b. Second Degree Murder:

      c. First Degree Murder:

      d. Hearing:

D. Parole violation (3000(d) & 3057 PC):

V. Probation (1202.7 – 1205.3 PC):
   A. Definition and Use (1202a PC):

   B. Legal Status (1203.1 PC):

   C. Eligibility for probation:

      1. Certain circumstances may make a defendant ineligible for probation, including:

         a. Armed with a firearm (1203(e)(2) or 1203.095) ("Use a Gun – Go to Jail" law)

         b. Use of a _____ (1203(e)(2) or 1203.095 PC)

         c. Causing _____ _____ (1203(e)(3) and 1203.075 PC

         d. Prior felony convictions (1203(e)(4) PC)

         e. Public official accepting a bribe or embezzling public funds (1203(e)(7) PC)

         f. Theft of over $ _____ (1203.06 PC)

      g. Certain crimes on public transit vehicles (1203.055 PC)

      h. Certain serious felonies (1203.6 PC) (Murder, robbery, kidnapping, first degree burglary, etc.)

      i. Certain sex crimes (1203.065, 1203.06 PC) (Rape, sodomy, etc.)

      j. Certain drug violations (1203.7 & .074 PC)

      k. Crimes against _____ (1202.09 PC)

  2. Authority of the court (1203e, 1203.095 (b & c) PC):

D. Probation Conditions (1203.04, 1203.1 – 1203.1k PC):
    1. Judge may order almost any reasonable conditions of probation:

    2. Rejection of Probation:

E. Length of Probation 1203a PC)

F. Summary Probation:

G. Probation Violation:

VI. Community Based Corrections Programs:
   A. Weekend sentence:

   B. Work furlough sentence:

   C. House Confinement (1203.015, 1203.016 PC):

   D. Diversion programs:

   E. Purpose of community based corrections:

VII. Effect of prior convictions in changing the classification of a crime (666, 647a PC etc.):

VIII. Juvenile Law:

   A. Age limitations:

   B. Juvenile death sentence (190.3a PC):

   C. Juvenile procedures:

Reading Assignment

1. California penal Code Sections:
    15 – 19d, 190.3a, 647a, 661, 667.5 – 667.10, 668, 669, 672, 1042.5, 1170 – 1170.95, 1192.7, 1202.7 –
    1205.3, 1208, 2930 – 2932, 3000 – 3065, 12022, 12022.5 & 12022.7.

Definitions

Define or explain the following:

1. statutory crimes:

2. common law crimes:

3. work furlough sentence:

4. public offense:

5. ex post facto:

6. felony:

7. misdemeanor:

8. optional crime:

9. infraction:

10. consecutive sentence:

11. concurrent sentence:

12. determinate sentence:

13. indeterminate sentence:

14. probation:

15. penalty enhancements:

California Habitual Criminal Laws

The California Habitual Criminal Laws are extremely complex. They have been enacted over an approximately 20-year period since 1976 to the present and have several overlapping provisions as well as conflicting court decisions regarding their application. Currently we have at least 12 different sections and subsections of the Penal Code which provide special penalties for habitual criminals.

PC Section	Prior Conviction	Current Conviction	Enhancement or Sentence	Enacted
667(a)(1) PC	Serious Felony	Serious Felony	5 years	1982
667.5(a) PC	Violent Felony w/i past 10 yrs.	Violent Felony	3 years	1976
667.5(b) PC	Any felony w/i past 5 years.	Any Felony	1 year	1976
667.51(a) PC	Any sex crime	Child Molesting	5 years	1981
667.51(b) PC	2 or more sex crimes	Child Molesting	15 yrs to life	1981
667.6(a) PC	Rape & other sex crimes w/i 10 yrs	Rape & other sex crimes	5 years	1979
667.6(b) PC	2 or more sex crimes w/i 10 yrs.	Rape & other sex crimes	10 years	1979
667.7(a)(1) PC	Served time on 2 violent felonies	Causes great bodily injury	Life (Parole in 20 years)	1981
667.7(a)(2) PC	Served time on 3 or more violent felonies	Causes great bodily injury	Life w/o parole	1981
667.71 PC (Habitual Sex Offender)	Rape or other violent sex crimes	Rape or other violent sex crime	25 to Life (Parole in 21 years)	1993
667.72 PC (Habitual Child Molester)	Served time for child molesting	Child Molesting	25 years (Parole in 20 years)	1993
667(b) to 667(i) (3 Strikes Law)	Served time for one prior violent felony conviction	Any felony	Double the sentence for current felony	1994
667(b) to 667(i) (3 Strikes Law)	Served time for two prior violent felony convictions	Any felony	Minimum 25 to Life	1994

Three Strikes Law (1994) (667 PC & 1170.12 PC):

The "Three Strikes" law, enacted in 1994, has complicated these sentencing provisions even further. The legislature created their version of the three strikes law and enacted it as an addition to 667 PC (667 (b) to (i))). The voter then passed Proposition 184 in November, 1994, with almost identical language. This was codified as section 1170.12 PC. Both the legislative version and the Prop. 184 version are in effect. The law provides a more severe sentence for any felony conviction, after having serve a prison sentence for any of the following prior serious felonies, as defined in 667.5 and 1192.7 PC:

    a. murder and attempted murder
    b. voluntary manslaughter
    c. rape
    d. kidnapping
    e. robbery
    f. ADW
    g. car jacking
    h. violent sex crimes
    i. residential burglary
    j. grand theft involving the use of a firearm
    k. selling drugs to a minor

Sentencing guidelines:

1. Prohibits probation or suspension of sentence.
2. Prohibits plea bargaining or striking prior felonies.
3. Requires state prison sentence.
4. All multiple sentences must run consecutively.

Note: When first enacted, these guidelines were mandatory and judges were required to adhere to them. In August, 1996, the California Supreme Court ruled that it was unconstitutional to impose such mandatory guidelines, therefore a judge may use the guidelines, but is not required to follow them.

Penalty:

1. With one prior violent felony conviction: Twice the normal sentence.

2. With two prior violent felony convictions: Life imprisonment, with a minimum sentence of:

    a. Three times the penalty prescribed for the current felony, **or**
    b. a minimum of 25 years, whichever is greater.

Chapter Problems:

A. Which of the following sentences would be legal and which would be illegal?

Use a penal code to find your answers and give code section numbers which support your answers.

1. Defendant convicted of disturbing the peace and sentenced to 180 days in county jail:

Illegal, ... 90 days

2. Defendant convicted of falsely impersonating a peace officer under section 538d PC and sentenced to one year in the county jail:

3. Defendant convicted of second degree burglary and sentenced to five days in the county jail:

Legal ...

B. Answer the following questions: (you may use the penal code)

1. A defendant is convicted of second degree burglary and sentenced to one year in the county jail.

   a. Has he been convicted of a felony or a misdemeanor?

2. A defendant is convicted of three counts of battery (242 PC). If he is sentenced to consecutive sentences in the county jail, what is the maximum time he could serve?

3. A defendant is convicted of petty theft in 1971 for stealing newspapers from a rack in front of a store and serves five days in the county jail. In 1975, he is again convicted of the same offense. What is the maximum punishment he could receive?

Penal Code 666, Petty ... (felony)

Chapter 3

Corpus Delicti and Legal Analysis

Introduction

Many legal terms have been so misused by the press and fiction writers that otherwise well-informed persons misinterpret words having precise legal definitions. This is particularly true of the Latin term "corpus Delicti" which some mystery writers continue to use to refer to the dead body in the hall closet.

This chapter defines and describes the legal significance of "corpus Delicti", "elements of crimes", "legal issues", "factual issues" and forms of evidence.

Objectives

When you complete this chapter you should be able to:

1. Describe the concept of dividing crimes into elements, including why it is done and how it affects proof of guilt in court.
2. Define "Corpus Delicti", describe its legal significance and recognize the elements of proof required in a typical criminal statute.
3. Define "Direct" and "Circumstantial" Evidence and describe their legal significance.
4. Distinguish between legal issues and factual issues and explain why enforcement procedures emphasize proof of facts rather than the legal requirements of the corpus Delicti.
5. Describe the analytical process and critical thinking needed to conduct a criminal investigation.

CORPUS DELICTI

A Programmed Lesson for Self-Instruction

This subject will be presented through use of a programmed lesson similar to the one used in Chapter 1. Again, you should follow the directions carefully. After each paragraph you will be asked a question and given a choice of answers. Your selection of an answer will lead you to a different page and paragraph. If you have difficulty in using this material, go back and reread the instructions at the beginning of Chapter 1

1. You have probably heard the legal term "Corpus Delicti" used in crime dramas on television or in the movies. Many mystery writers have used the phrase in courtroom scenes for its pseudo-legalistic effect. While most are correct in its usage, some are still inclined to hide the "Corpus Delicti" in the hall closet, although the term has nothing to do with dead bodies.

   Go on to paragraph 2.

2. The term "corpus Delicti" refers to the elements in the definition of a crime. The "elements" are those factors which must exist in order to establish that the crime has occurred. All of the elements of a crime, taken together, constitute the Corpus Delicti of that crime. The Corpus Delicti of a crime forms a checklist of the requirements that must be satisfied in order to prove that the crime has occurred. If any single element of the corpus Delicti is missing, then the crime has not taken place.

   Turn to paragraph 7.

3. No, sorry, you're wrong. "Corpus" is not the right answer. The correct answer is "element."

   Turn to paragraph 12.

4. No, that's not true. Every crime is composed of elements and every crime has a "corpus Delicti"; not just the crime of murder.

   Go on to paragraph 5.

5. True or False?

   The "corpus Delicti" in a murder refers to producing the dead body of the victim.

   If your answer is true, turn to paragraph 27.
   If your answer is false, turn to paragraph 10.

6. No. Sorry, but you're wrong again. The number of elements in the corpus Delicti will vary from one crime to another.

   That makes three wrong answers in a row.

   Better go back to paragraph 2 and reread slowly and carefully from that point.
   Follow directions carefully as you read.

7. Each part of a crime is called:

   1. A corpus Delicti.   (Don't forget to circle the correct answer on
   2. An element.   The answer sheet also.)
   3. A proof.
   4. A corpus.

   If 1 is correct, turn to paragraph 16.   If 3 is correct, turn to paragraph 22.
   If 2 is correct, turn to paragraph 21.   If 4 is correct, turn to paragraph 3.

8.	No. You will have to prove each and every element of the crime in order to establish that a criminal act has taken place. If any one element is missing in your proof, then you cannot convict the defendant because you cannot show that a crime has occurred. Turn to paragraph 14.

9.	True or False?
	
	Murder is the only crime which has a corpus delicti.
	
	        If your answer is true, turn to paragraph 4.
	        If your answer is false, turn to paragraph 18.

10.	Correct. The corpus delicti actually has nothing to do with the dead body. Although in a criminal homicide you will have to prove that the victim died, this can be done either with or without finding the body of the victim. Go on to paragraph 11.

11.	True or False?
	
	All crimes have the same number of elements in the corpus Delicti.
	
	        If your answer is true, turn to paragraph 33.
	        If your answer is false, turn to paragraph 31.

12.	To see what is meant by the term "elements," let's look at an example of a crime definition. The crime of "Burglary" is defined as "entering a building with the intention of stealing something or committing a felony." Every burglary has three separate and distinct parts which must be proven in order to show that a crime has taken place.
	
	        First – "That a person has entered" …
	        Second – "a building" …
	        Third – "with the intent of committing a theft or some felony."
	
	In order to convict a person of burglary you must prove the existence of all three of the above elements. If any one is missing, then you have not established that a burglary has occurred.
	
	        Turn to paragraph 17.

13.	Correct. In order to prove that a crime has taken place, you must prove each and every element of the crime. If any single element is missing, you will not even be able to present your case to the jury, as the elements must be established right at the start of your case. Go on to paragraph 14.

14. The term "corpus delicti" means all the parts or "elements" of a crime. Sometimes this is called the "body of the crime," although it has nothing to do with the dead body in a murder case. Every crime is composed of elements, and every crime has a "corpus delicti," which simply means all of the elements of that crime. The "corpus delicti" of some crimes consists of only two or three elements while others may have as many as seven or eight elements.

    Turn to paragraph 9.

15. True or False?

    All crimes have the same number of elements in the corpus delicti

    If your answer is true, turn to paragraph 6.
    If your answer is false, turn to paragraph 25

16. No, sorry, you're wrong. "Corpus delicti" isn't the name given for each part of the crime. The correct answer is "element."

    Go on to paragraph 12.

17. If the definition of a crime consists of three elements, the proof of how many of the three will be necessary in order to convict the guilty party?

    1. Prove any one of the three.
    2. Prove all three of the elements.
    3. Prove as many elements as possible and let the jury decide if you have presented enough to convince them.

    If 1 is correct, turn to paragraph 8.
    If 2 is correct, turn to paragraph 13.
    If 3 is correct, turn to paragraph 23.

18. Right! Every crime is composed of elements and has a corpus delicti; not just the crime of murder.

    Go on to paragraph 19.

19. True or False?

    The corpus delicti in a murder refers to producing the dead body of the victim.

    If your answer is true, turn to paragraph 24.
    If your answer is false, turn to paragraph 10.

20. No. Sorry, but that's the wrong answer. The number of elements in the corpus delicti will vary from one crime to another.

    You've just missed two questions in a row.
    How about going back to paragraph 14 and rereading from there. Read the material slowly and be certain that you understand it.

21. Right. Element is the word used to define each part of a crime. Let's go on and look at an example of some elements.

Turn to paragraph 12.

22. No, sorry, you're wrong. "Proof" is not the right answer. The correct answer is "element."

Turn to paragraph 12.

23. No. You will have to prove each and every element of the crime in order to establish that a criminal act has taken place. You will have to do this at the start of your case or you will never get far enough to let the jury hear any of your other evidence.

Turn to paragraph 14.

24. No, that's not right. The word "corpus delicti" actually has nothing to do with the dead body. In a criminal homicide you will have to prove that the victim died, but this can be done either with or without the body.

Turn to paragraph 28.

25. Good. You had a little trouble for a question or two but now you're back on track again. You're right; the number of elements in the corpus delicti will vary from one crime to another.

Turn to paragraph 34.

26. Nope, you can't do it. Go back to paragraph 32 and reread answer 3 until it looks right (cause it is) and then continue on to paragraph 35 from there.

27. No, that's not right. The word "corpus delicti" actually has nothing to do with the dead body. In a criminal homicide you will have to prove that the victim died, but this can be done either with or without the body.

You've just missed two questions in a row. Perhaps you should read a little more carefully.

Turn to paragraph 30.

28. True or False?

All crimes have the same number of elements in the corpus delicti.

If your answer is true, turn to paragraph 20.
If your answer is false, turn to paragraph 25.

29. Let's say that you're a desk officer on duty at your local police department. While you're enjoying your third cup of coffee of the morning, a man suddenly runs in and shouts that he wants to confess a crime which has been on his conscience for 10 years. He proceeds to tell you all the gory details about how he killed his Aunt Minnie ten years before. He repeats the confession for a stenographer after being advised of his rights and then sight it … a perfectly valid, legal confession.

(continue on to the next page)

Now, these are the elements of a criminal homicide: first, that a person was once alive; second, that that person is now dead; and third, that the death was caused by the criminal act of another.

After taking the confession you conduct an investigation to establish all of these elements. First, you prove that Minnie was once a live person by finding birth certificates, employment records, relatives, and friends who knew her, and things like that. Then, you prove that she is now dead by locating a death certificate, the doctor who pronounced her dead, and the funeral director who buried her. So far, so good. But now you come to a problem. The death certificate says she died of old age complicated by an overly developed fondness for fermented grape juice. In short, she died from being an alcoholic; not from being hit on the head by a shovel as your suspect has stated in his confession. So you even have Minnie's body dug up at Shady Nook cemetery but still cannot show that she died from anything other than natural causes. What will happen to your case against the suspect if he decides to plead "not guilty"?

Turn to paragraph 32.

30. (NOTE: This is a repetition of paragraph 14.)

The term "corpus delicti" means all of the parts or "elements" of a crime. Sometimes this is called the "body of the crime," although it has nothing to do with a dead body in a murder case. Every crime is composed of elements, and every crime has a corpus delicti, which simply means, all of the elements of that crime. The corpus delicti of some crimes consists of only tow or three elements while others have as many as seven or eight elements.

Remember that the phrase "corpus delicti" is not limited to just homicides, but that every crime has a corpus delicti.

Also, don't forget that the corpus delicti doesn't mean the dead body of the victim.

Turn to paragraph 15.

31. That's right.

Continue on to paragraph 34.

32. What will happen to your case? Choose one of the answers below.

1. You will still convict him because "corpus delicti" means "dead body" and as long as Minnie has been dug up, you have established the corpus delicti.
2. As long as the suspect has confessed, the jury will probably accept his confession and convict him.
3. You will never bring the case to trial because you have failed to establish the third element of the corpus delicti and without a corpus delicti the defendant's confession can't be used.

If your answer is 1 go back and pick another answer.
If your answer is 2, turn to paragraph 26.
If your answer is 3, turn to paragraph 35.

33. No, sorry, but that's wrong. You've been doing quite well though so don't feel badly.

Actually, the number of elements in the corpus delicti will vary from one crime to another. There is no set figure although it will usually be between three and six elements.

Go on to paragraph 34.

34. There are several reasons why we use the ideas of "elements" and "corpus delicti" in defining criminal acts. First, it makes it easier to study law by providing a simple outline description of every crime; it also makes it easier to determine if a particular law has been violated because it provides a checklist of the things that must occur in order for a crime to be committed. If we suspect that someone has violated a law, we simply go down the checklist and see if all of the elements of that crime have taken place. If any element is missing, then a crime hasn't occurred, and if there has been no crime then we can't convict someone of committing that crime. It's that simple.

Another important factor about corpus delicti is that we cannot use a defendant's admission or confession against him in court unless we first establish the corpus delicti of the crime. If we cannot establish all of the elements of the crime apart from his confession, then we cannot convict him.

Turn to paragraph 29.

35. Right. You can't prove that a crime has taken place unless you can establish all of the elements of that crime. One of the elements of a criminal homicide is that the victim died from the criminal act of another. If you can't show that Minnie died from some criminal act of another, then you haven't established all the elements of the corpus delicti. And until you do, that confession will never reach the jury.

Turn to paragraph 36.

36. Another Latin legal term, which we hear frequently, is "prima facie" (pronounced pry-muh fay-shuh). The literal translation of prima facie is "on its face," meaning "at first appearance." In law it is used to describe the basic case which the prosecution must present in court. A prima Facie case consists of two parts: first, the prosecution must establish the corpus delicti of the crime, and second, they must present reasonable evidence of the defendant's guilt. This is considered to be a prima facie case and it shifts the burden of going forward with the case to the defendant. The defendant now must produce evidence to show his innocence. The principal that the defendant is considered innocent until proven guilty is an important part of our law, but somewhere in the trial, a point is reached where the defendant can no longer rely on the presumption of innocence but must produce some evidence in his own behalf. That point is reached when the prosecutor has established a prima facie case. That is when "on its face" it appears that the defendant is guilty. The defendant must then offer his or her own evidence to answer the prosecutor's evidence.

Turn to paragraph 39.

37. Right again. If the prosecution has established a satisfactory prima facie case, and the defendant offer nothing to contradict it, then the prosecution should win the case because the presumption of innocence has been overcome.

> Go on to paragraph 46.

38. Certain questions will frequently arise concerning circumstantial evidence.

For example: can a person be convicted of a crime solely on circumstantial evidence?

> Write your answer here: _____ and turn to paragraph 43.
> (yes or no)

39. In a criminal prosecution, the D. A. proves that a burglary has taken place. He then produces evidence that appears to reasonably prove that the defendant committed the burglary. At the close of the D. A.'s presentation, the defendant is asked to present his defense. He refuses, claiming that he is not required to say anything or produce any evidence if he doesn't want to. If the trial ends at this point, which side should win the case?

1. The prosecution, because the defendant cannot refuse to testify in his own behalf.
2. The defendant, because he cannot be forced to present evidence if he doesn't want to.
3. The prosecution, because they have established a prima facie case and the defendant has not gone forward with his defense.

> If your answer is 1, turn to paragraph 42.
> If your answer is 2, turn to paragraph 45.
> If your answer is 3, turn to paragraph 37.

40. The answer to 43 is **"YES,"** a defendant can be convicted of murder on just circumstantial evidence.

In murder, as in many other crimes, it is common that there are no eyewitnesses and no confession. Without circumstantial physical evidence, many defendants who are obviously guilty would not be convicted.

Can a defendant be convicted of first-degree murder solely on circumstantial evidence and without finding the body of the victim?

> Write your answer here _____ and turn to paragraph 44.
> (yes or no)

41. The answer to 44 is **"YES,"** a defendant can be convicted of first degree murder and receive a death sentence without the victim's body ever being recovered and where the only evidence is what would be classified as circumstantial evidence.

Although it is legally possible to receive a death sentence under these circumstances, it is highly unlikely and, to my knowledge, has never occurred. L. Ewing Scott, although convicted of first-degree murder, received a life sentence rather than a death sentence.

> Turn to paragraph 47.

42. You're correct that the prosecution should win the case, but it's not because the defendant cannot refuse to testify. A defendant can never be forced to testify or produce any evidence if he doesn't want to however, if the prosecution has established a satisfactory prima facie case and the defendant offers nothing to contradict it, then the prosecution should win the case because the presumption of innocence has been overcome.

Answer 3 was correct for paragraph 39.

Go on to paragraph 46.

43. The answer to 38 is **"YES,"** a defendant can be convicted solely on circumstantial evidence.

Can a defendant be convicted of murder on circumstantial evidence alone?

Write your answer here _____ and turn to paragraph 40.
(yes or no)

44. The answer to 40 is **"YES,"** a defendant can legally be convicted of first-degree murder solely on circumstantial evidence and without finding the body of the victim. A leading case of this type was that of People vs. L. Ewing Scott (176 CA2 458). In this case, Mr. Scott's wife disappeared. He was accused of killing her although her body was never found. Part of the evidence produced against him consisted of the fact that he had forged her name to several documents in order to gain control of her property immediately after she disappeared. He also delayed several days before notifying anyone of her disappearance. Some of Mrs. Scott's personal jewelry was found buried in his backyard and her false teeth were found in his incinerator. All of the evidence was sufficient to convince a jury that he had killed her and he was convicted of first-degree murder although all the evidence was circumstantial and Mrs. Scott's body was never found. Many years later, after completing his sentence, he finally confessed to the crime.

Can a defendant be convicted of first degree murder and receive a death sentence if the body of the victim is never found?

Write your answer here _____ and turn to paragraph 41.
(yes or no)

45. It's true that the defendant cannot be forced to testify or produce evidence if he doesn't want to but if the prosecution has established a satisfactory prima facie case and the defendant offers nothing to contradict it, then the prosecution should win the case because the presumption of innocence has been overcome.

Answer 3 w3as correct for paragraph 39.

Go on to paragraph 46.

46. One other legal term, which is used quite frequently by the news media, is "circumstantial evidence." Unfortunately, this term has acquired an unsavory connotation. You frequently read or hear that the evidence against a defendant is "only circumstantial."

   Most criminals are convicted on the basis of circumstantial evidence and frequently circumstantial evidence is more reliable than other types of evidence. Circumstantial evidence can be defined as "evidence which proves a fact indirectly, by inference from other facts." It usually means any evidence other than eyewitness or a confession. Anything other than someone who actually saw the defendant commit the crime or a confession from the criminal himself is simply "circumstantial." But if the circumstantial evidence consists of fingerprints or other physical evidence acquired by laboratory methods, its validity and accuracy are far more certain than that of the eyewitness. Some types of physical evidence have an accuracy of well over 99% while eyewitnesses can be wrong in more than 50% of what they think they see.

   Turn to paragraph 38.

47. That's it. You have now completed the programmed lesson on "Corpus Delicti."

   Be sure to complete the definitions and questions at the end of the chapter. If you have any questions be certain to ask the instructor to explain anything you don't understand.

Program Study Notes

For study purposes, the paragraphs in this programmed lesson may be read in the following order:

1
2
12
14
34
36
46
38
43
40
44
41

Following the order given above will allow you to skip the paragraphs which merely provide directions and will permit you to read only the paragraphs containing factual information.

Do *not* follow this outline for your initial study of the lesson. It is very important that you proceed according to directions the first time through in order to achieve the full benefit of programmed learning methods.

Remember; don't use this outline until you have first completed the topic in the manner described in the instructions.

LECTURE NOTES OUTLINE:

I.   Corpus Delicti and Elements of crimes (review of programmed lesson):
     A. General

     B. Examples of Corpus Delicti and Elements:
         1. Burglary (459PC):

             (a)

             (b)

             (c)

         2. Theft (Larceny) (484PC):

             (a)

             (b)

             (c)

             (d)

II.   Legal Reasoning and Analysis:
        A.   Steps of Analysis:
             1. *Reconstruct* facts of incident from reliable sources:

                a. Accurate, complete facts may not always be available:

             2. *Identify Relevant Law*:

                a. Research both _____ law and the _____ law.

             3. *Compare and match* facts of case to elements of the corpus delicti:

             4. Identify relevant *legal issues*:

             5. Consider *possible alternatives* and reach *appropriate decisions*:
                a. Reporting Officer:

                b. Investigator:

                c. DA:

                d. Discretionary judgment:

III. Examples of matching facts to elements of a crime:
 A. Person goes into a store to shop, sees an item on a counter, gets tempted and takes it.
    Guilty of burglary?

 B. Person goes into a store intending to steal but can't find anything, Leaves without taking anything.
    Guilty of burglary?

IV. Legal Issues vs. Factual Issues:
 A. Legal Issues:

 B. Factual Issues:

Class Question: In shoplifting, when is the theft completed?

Class Question: A person enters a store to shop, sees a camera on the counter and decides to steal it. He picks it up from the counter, puts it in a pocket, walks out of the camera department, out the main entrance of the store and is stopped by store security in the parking lot

When was the theft of the camera completed?

Definitions

Define or explain the following:

A. corpus delicti:

B. prima facie case:

C. circumstantial evidence

Chapter Questions

1. What is the significance of establishing the corpus delicti in relation to the admission of a defendant's confession in court?

2. Explain the significance of the case of People vs. L. Ewing Scott, 176 CA2 458, described in the programmed lesson.

3. Give two reasons why crimes are divided into elements:

4. Compare legal issues and factual issues and explain why it is important to be able to understand the differences between the two.

Chapter 4

Act and Intent

Introduction

A crime can be committed either by doing something which is prohibited by law or by failing to do something which is required by law. In either case, the act (or failure to act) must be accompanied by a wrongful intent in order to be a crime. A mere intent to do something wrong is not a crime unless some action is taken to carry out the intent. Likewise, an accident which results in injury to someone is not a crime unless it was done with some form of criminal intent or criminal negligence. This chapter examines the concept of joint operation of act and intent, and also the effect of motive and intoxication on the commission of a crime

Objectives

Upon completing this chapter, you should be able to:

1. Recognize legal problems involving proof of intent in criminal cases; distinguishing between general, specific and transferred criminal intents and explain the concept of proximate cause.
2. Distinguish between motive and intent.
3. Describe the effect of intoxication on responsibility for a criminal act.

Lecture Notes Outline

I. Necessity of joint union of act and intent (PC20)

II. The criminal act:
   A. Affirmative acts:

B. Failure to act:

    1. Requirement of Duty:

        a. Legal theories of imposing a duty:
          (1) Prior Actions:

          (2) Relationship:

          (3) Employment:

C. Act or failure to act must satisfy the elements of a criminal statute:

D. Proximate cause:
    1. Definition:

    2. Existence of proximate cause determined by the _____.

    3. Standards for determining proximate cause:

E. Multiple causation:

III. Intent

   A. Definition of an intentional act:

   B. Intent vs. Motive:
       1. Motive:

       2. Intent:

       Example:

   C. Rules of evidence:

   D. Types of Intent:

       1. General intent:
          a. Presumption:

          b. Negligence:

c. Lack of both intent and negligence:

2. Specific intent:
   a. Description:

   b. Proof of intent:

   c. Transferred intent:

D. Effect of intoxication on criminal responsibility (PC22):
   1. Voluntary intoxication:
      a. General rule:

      b. Diminished capacity exception:

   2. Involuntary intoxication:

Reading Assignment

1. California Penal Code Sections: 20, 21 and 22

Definitions

Define or explain the following:

A. proximate cause:

B. multiple causation:

C. general intent:

D. specific intent:

E. transferred intent:

F. motive:

G. reasonably foreseeable:

Act and Intent Problems

The act and intent concept is one of the most difficult legal principles to understand. It is a concept on which experienced attorneys will frequently disagree. Many legal volumes and hundreds of case opinions have been written in an attempt to clarify this confusing area of the law.

Much of the problem arises from the broad definitions which must be applied to terms such as "proximate cause," "reasonable," and "negligent." Also remember that their application in a particular case is left to the discretion of a jury which will be affected by factors such as the seriousness of the offense involved and the personalities of the particular defendant and victim.

Instructions for Use of Act and Intent Checklist

It's not possible to develop a mechanical formula which can be applied to every type of crime to automatically resolve the problems of act and intent. The following guide may be useful however in solving problems of act and intent in some crimes which involve injury to a victim or damage to his property.

It is a step-by-step checklist which will guide you through all the pertinent factors in act and intent problems.

CHECKLIST FOR RESOLVING
ACT AND INTENT PROBLEMS

Establishing Actual Cause ☐
1. Did some act or failure by the defendant result in an injury or loss to the victim? If the defendant's actions were not the cause of the victim's injury, then he is not guilty. If the defendant's actions did cause injury or damage to the victim, go on to question 2.

Establishing Proximate Cause ☐
2. Was the defendant's conduct the proximate cause of the victim's injury (Was the result reasonably direct or reasonably foreseeable or originally intended by the defendant?). If not, the defendant is not guilty. If proximate cause exists, go on to number 3

Establishing an Act or Failure to Act ☐
3. Did the defendant take some deliberate, affirmative action against the victim or was the victim's injury caused because the defendant failed to act? If it was an affirmative act go directly to question 6. If the victim was injured because the defendant failed to do something, go on to question 4.

Establishing A Duty to Act ☐
4. If the victim's injury was caused because of something the defendant failed to do, was the defendant required to take action (statute, prior act or def., relationship to victim, contract for care of victim)? If he was not legally required to take action, then he is not guilty. If he was required to act but failed to do so, go on to question 5.

Establishing an Ability and Awareness to Act ☐
5. Was it physically possible for the defendant to act and was he aware of the need for action? If he was not aware of such need and his lack of knowledge was not due to his own negligence, or if it was not possible for him to take action, he is not guilty. If he was aware of the need and capable of acting, go on to question 6.

Establishing Violation of a Criminal Statute ☐
6. Does a criminal statute exist for the type of injury caused to the victim? If the defendant's actions have not satisfied the corpus delicti of a crime, then he is not guilty. If the elements of a crime have been satisfied, continue on to question 7.

Establishing need for Specific Criminal Intent ☐
7. Does the statute require a specific intent? If not, go to question 9. If it is a specific statute, go to question 8.

Establishing Defendant's Specific Intent ☐
8. If the law requires a specific intent, did the defendant have such necessary intent? If not, he is not guilty. If he did have the required intent, he is guilty of that crime.

Establishing a General Criminal Intent ☐
9. Was the defendant's conduct brought about as a deliberate, conscious act or was it an unintentional accident? If it was accidental he may not be guilty. Go to the next question.

Establishing Negligence In Lieu of General Intent ☐
10. If the defendant's act was unintentional was he acting in a negligent manner? If so, he may be guilty even though he did not deliberately intend to cause injury or loss to the victim. On the other hand, if his conduct was reasonable, lawful and not negligent, then he is not guilty of a crime even though he may have caused death, injury or loss to the victim.

Chapter Problems

In each of the following problems decide whether the defendant is guilty or not guilty of the crime charged. Your decision should be based on the rules relating to crime causation and act and intent. Give a brief explanation of your reason for each decision. For the purpose of these problems you may use the following definitions of the statute on murder and manslaughter:

Murder: "A death brought about as a result of some conduct by the defendant done with the specific intent to kill the victim."

Manslaughter: "A death brought about by some conduct by the defendant done with negligence or wrongful purpose or without reasonable care for the safety of others but without an intent to kill."

If you have difficulty, use the checklist on the previous page. Record answers on the Answer Sheet to submit as homework.

1. Archie is driving through a residential area with his girlfriend, Beatrice. As he is driving he momentarily takes his eyes from the road as he leans over to kiss Beatrice. Because of this, he fails to see a stop sign posted at an intersection and collides with another car resulting in the death of the other driver

   Is Archie guilty of manslaughter? _____

   Legal reasoning:

2. Albert is driving at about 25 MPH in an unfamiliar residential area and approaches an intersection. He sees another vehicle approaching from his left and he slows down to about 15 MPH. He does not intend to stop because he knows that the vehicle entering an uncontrolled intersection from the right has the right of way and that the other vehicle should stop. Too late, he realizes that the other vehicle is not going to stop. He applies his brakes but cannot stop in time and the other driver is killed. He later learns that the other driver continued through because the intersection is signal controlled and the victim had a green light. Albert could not see the single red light facing him because it was completely obscured by low hanging branches and was invisible from his side of the road.

   Is Albert guilty of manslaughter? _____

   Legal reasoning:

3. Bruce is driving on the Santa Ana Freeway at approximately 60 MPH. Traffic suddenly slows down in front of him and he sees several cars in front swing out to pass an old car traveling at 45 MPH in the left lane. He is caught behind the car and after following it for several minutes attempting to pass; he lightly taps his horn, hoping to get the other driver to pull to the right. The driver of the other car is an elderly gentleman who is startled by the sound of the horn behind him, loses control of his vehicle, strikes the guardrail, and is killed.

   Is Bruce guilty of manslaughter? _____

   Legal reasoning:

4. Bertram is a nineteen-year-old college student. He likes to move fast and has a lilac T-Bird with a loud air horn. While driving to school he stops at an intersection for a red light. An old man starts across the street in front of Bert and reaches the front of Bert's car just as the light changes to green for Bert. The man becomes confused at the change of lights and hesitates in front of Bert's car. Bert, intending to have some fun by scaring the man, gives a loud blast on the air horn. This so startles the man that he runs in front of a car in the other lane and is killed.

   Is Bertram guilty of manslaughter? _____

   Legal reasoning:

5. Bertram parks in a drive-in in his lilac T-Bird. In order to attract the attention of the waitress, he gives a loud blast on his air horn. The noise startles a cook in the kitchen who jumps up, knocking over a shelf of spices. A box of crushed red pepper falls into a vat of strawberry pancake batter being mixed by the cook. About twenty minutes later, Sydney comes in and orders strawberry pancakes. When they are served, he takes a large bite. The pain from the pepper causes him to gasp and he chokes to death on the pancake.

   Is Bertram guilty of manslaughter? _____

   Legal reasoning:

4-9

6. Arthur intends to kill Benson with a rifle. He hides in a window of an apartment building across from Benson's office. When Benson leaves his office, Arthur takes careful aim with the rifle and is about to pull the trigger when he sees a truck speeding down the street. Arthur could shout and warn Benson but he does not. Benson is struck and killed by the truck.

    Is Arthur guilty of either murder or manslaughter? _____

    Legal reasoning:

7. Sam is in love with Irving's wife, Sybil. Together with Sybil he plans a method of killing Irving so that Sybil will be free to marry him. With Sybil's help he puts the following plan into effect. Irving is an alcoholic and always becomes extremely intoxicated at parties. Sam decides to give a series of parties at which he will allow Irving to get drunk so that the other guests will learn of Irving's fondness for alcohol and inability to care for himself when drinking. He is certain that after his friends observe Irving's condition at a few of these parties they would conclude that any accident resulting in Irving's death was caused by his drunken condition and no one would suspect murder. He then intends to allow Irving to get drunk and jostle him over the edge of a balcony railing in an apparent accident. Even with guests standing close by, he is certain that they will believe that they have witnessed an accident caused by Irving's drunken condition. All goes well at the first of these parties and the desired impression is made on the guests. At the second party, Irving again proceeds to get drunk as expected. By midnight, Irving is in a drunken stupor and prepares to leave. Sam tries to help him into his coat. At that moment, a guest standing behind Sam stumbles and falls against him. Sam makes every effort to keep his balance but is pushed against Irving accidentally. The drunken Irving falls headlong down a flight of stairs and dies in a hospital the next day because of his injuries. The elated Sam and Sybil marry two months later.

    Is Sam guilty of either murder or manslaughter? _____

    Legal reasoning:

8. Milton and Bruce are driving down Pico Blvd. in Milton's brand new lilac Mustang, enroute to a party in Beverly Hills. As they approach Sepulveda Blvd. Milton turns to Bruce and says, "Bruce, I just don't know what I'm going to do. These brakes don't seem to be working properly." Bruce, who is the brighter of the two, suggests that they pull into a garage and have them checked. Milton agrees and stops at the next gas station, which, fortunately, provides the services of a brake mechanic. The mechanic is able to repair the brakes and gives Milton a brake inspection certificate showing that his brakes are in proper working order. Milton tests the brakes as they leave the garage and they seem to be working. Three blocks later the brakes fail completely because of a faulty hydraulic line. The car slides into an intersection, strikes another vehicle, and kills the other driver.

    Is Milton guilty of either murder or manslaughter? _____

    Explain your answer fully.

9. Louise works as a home nurse for an elderly, bed-ridden patient. One evening, after seeing that the patient was asleep, she leaves the house to carry out some personal business, even though her instructions are to remain within hearing distance of the patient's room at all times, because of his fragile condition. While she is gone a violent rainstorm comes up. The elderly gentleman attempts to call her when rain begins to pour through the open window. When she does not respond, he tries to close the window himself but collapses from the exertion. Louise returns two hours later to find him dead on the floor.

Is she guilty of either murder or manslaughter? _____

Explain your answer.

10. Dangerous Dan is a hired killer. He accepts a job to assassinate a union official for a price of $10,000. In carrying out the crime, he breaks into the victim's bedroom, discovers the victim in bed, and fires 3 shots into the sleeping body. A later autopsy proves that the victim did not die as a result of the gunshot wounds. The victim was actually already dead when the shots were fired, having died in his sleep from a heart attack an hour before.

Is the defendant guilty of murder? _____

Is he guilty of manslaughter? _____

Explain you answer.

Chapter 5

Parties to a Crime

Introduction

Whenever two or more people take part in a criminal venture, they share degrees of responsibility for the results of their crimes. The extent of the participation will vary for each individual. One may act as a lookout; one may assist only in the planning; another may actually commit the criminal act; which still another may hid the fleeing fugitives from the police

In this chapter you will learn to determine the extent of legal responsibility of each of these participants.

Objectives

Upon completing this chapter, you should be able to:

1. Explain the rules relating to legal responsibility of participants in a criminal activity, including conspirators, principals, accomplices, accessories, solicitors and compounders.
2. Given the facts of a criminal case, including the actions of each of several parties, be able to determine the criminal responsibilities of each

Lecture Notes Outline

I. General Rule:

II. Principals (31PC):

   A. Definition:

      1. Personally committing the crime: (First method with three variations)
       a. Directly satisfying elements of crime through his or her own actions: (First Variation)

b.   Committing crime by use of an instrument: (Second Variation)

c.   Committing crime by use of an agent: (Third Variation)

2. Aids, abets, advises or encourages: (Second method of becoming a principal)
  a.   Participation:

b.   Knowledge

C. Significant results of being a principal:
  1. Guilty though not present or not the actual perpetrator (vicarious liability):

a. People vs. Le Grant, 76 CA2 148

b. People vs. Wood, 56 CA 431

2. Guilty though legally incapable of committing a particular crime:

3. Responsibility for reasonably foreseeable results:

    a. Period of Responsibility:

4. Guilty though major wrongdoer has a defense:

D. Withdrawal from status of principal:
  1. Requirements:

    a.

    b.

  2. Responsibility for prior crimes:

E. Criminal charges:

III. Accessories (32PC):
   A. General Definition:

   B. Elements and analysis:
      1. Action element:

      2. Knowledge element:

      3. Intent element:

   C. Penalty (33 PC):

IV. Accomplices (1111 PC):
   A. Definition:

   B. Significance:

   C. Feigned Accomplices:

V. Soliciting (653f PC):
   A. Definition:

   B. MR. F. K. BERRGAPAA:

     M –
     R –
     F –
     K –
     B –
     E –
     R –
     R –
     G –
     A –
     P –
     A –
     A –

   C. Intent:

   D. Commission of intended crime:

   E. Corroboration:

   F. Penalty:

VI. Compounding a crime (153 PC):
   A. Definition:

B. Elements:
   1.

   2.

   3.

C. Penalty:

VII. Conspiracy (182 PC):
   A. Introduction:

   B. Elements:
     1. An _____

     2. between _____ persons,

     3. to commit a _____ ,

     4. coupled with _____ .

C. Responsibility:

D. Withdrawal from conspiracy:

.

E. Penalty:

VIII. Employer – employee liability:

A. Civil liability:

B. Employer may be criminally responsible under the following conditions:

1.

2.

3.

5-7

Reading Assignment

1. California Penal Code Sections.
   1. Principals:
      Penal Code Sections: 30 – 33 & 971
   2. Employer - employee
      No Code Sections.
   3. Accessories:
      Penal Code Sections: 30, 32 & 33
   4. Accomplices:
      Penal Code Section: 1111
   5. Soliciting:
      Penal Code Section: 653f
   6. Compounding:
      Penal Code Section: 153 & 1377 – 1379
   7. Conspiracy:
      Penal Code Sections: 182 – 184

Definitions

Define or explain the following:

A. principal:

B. aid and abet:

C. accessory:

D. accomplice:

E. corroboration:

F. soliciting a crime:

G. compounding a crime:

H. conspiracy:

J. overt act:

Chapter Problems

In each of the following problems, determine whether the defendant is a party to a crime in any way, and if so, what crimes and under what theory. Explain fully.

1. Charlie is walking near his home when he sees three men beating an old enemy of his. He watches from the opposite sidewalk but does nothing more. He does not call the police.

2. Assume the same facts as in problem 1 except Charlie shouts across the street, "Hit him again for me," then runs across the street to shout encouragement. The assailants are about to run off, but at Charlie's urging, continue the beating for several more minutes.

3. You plan to hold up a bank with several friends. On the day before the holdup you call one of the friends and tell him you don't think it will work and that you are dropping out. They go ahead with the robbery, are trapped, and kill a bank clerk in their getaway

   Of what crimes are you guilty?

4. Two teenage friends tell you of their plan to steal some beer at a liquor store. They ask you to drive a car as part of the plan. You believe them and go along. While you park down a side street, they rob the liquor store instead of stealing beer. They kill a clerk during the crime. They do not tell you of the crime until a half hour after you have driven them from the scene. You then call the police.

   Of what crimes are you guilty?

5. You want to do away with you mother-in-law and ask your best friend Larry to slip her some arsenic. He refuses.

   Are you guilty of a crime?

   Is Larry?

6. Larry agrees to slip the arsenic to your mother-in-law but after driving around for two hours he cannot find her house and comes back.

   Are you guilty of a crime?

   Is Larry?

7. Satchel Sam joins the Murphy gang in planning a bank robbery. Sam is to drive the getaway car. He buys a fast car from his brother Alex to be used in the job. Before they can attempt the stickup, the Murphy gang drops out and the whole plan is forgotten.

   Is Sam guilty of a crime?

8. Boris Kusnov joins Sam and his brother Alex in replanning the bank holdup. Boris is to drive the getaway car and he is impressed with the one car, which Sam purchased, and a second one, which was stolen before Boris, joined them and which was to be used as a second getaway car. Boris convinces his friend, Nikolai, to join them in the robbery. All goes as planned during the robbery; however, when they escape in the two cars, the police pursue the one containing Sam and Alex. Boris and Nikolai escape but Sam is in a collision while being chased and Alex is killed in the accident.

   Of what crimes is Boris guilty?

History of Principals and Accessories

There are only two classifications of persons involved in the commission of crimes in California: (1) principals; and (2) accessories. The term "principal" refers to all parties involved in the commission of a crime, whether felon or misdemeanor, while the term "accessory" refers only to parties giving aid after the commission of a felony. There is no such thing as an accessory to a misdemeanor in California (Sec. 32 PC).

Under early common law, parties to a crime were divided into (1) principals of the first degree; (1) principals of the second degree; (3) accessories before the fact; and (4) accessories after the fact.

A "principal of the first degree" was the person who actually committed the crime, such as the one who struck the fatal blow in a murder, the one who entered the building in a burglary, the one who physically carried away the victim in a kidnapping or who actually performed whatever wrongful act was necessary to commit the particular crime.

A "principal in the second degree" was one who was present at the scene and who aided and abetted the perpetrator, but did not actually commit the crime. Principals of the first and second degree were equally guilty and subject to identical punishments.

An "accessory before the fact" was one who counseled, aided, commanded, procured or other wise encouraged the guilty party to commit the crime, but who was not present at the actual commission of the offense. He, also, was equally guilty and subject to the same punishment as the principal in the first or second degree.

According to the procedural rules existing at that time, a conviction was not possible if the defendant was charged as a principal and proved to be an accessory, or was charged as an accessory and proved to be a principal. Also, accessories and second-degree principals could not be tried until after the conviction of the first degree principal. If the principal was never apprehended or had died, the others could not be brought to justice. It became apparent that it was highly desirable to eliminate entirely the distinction between principals of the first degree, principals of the second degree and accessories before the fact and declare all such parties to be principals. The California legislature did just that in 1880 by amending section 971 of the Penal Code, which reads as follows:

"The distinction between an accessory before the fact and a principal, and between principals in the first and second degree is abrogated; and all persons concerned in the commission of a crime, who by the operation of other provisions of this code are principals therein, shall hereafter be prosecuted, tried, and punished as principals and no other facts need be alleged in any accusatory pleading against any such person than are required in an accusatory pleading against a principal."

Chapter 6

Laws of Arrest

Introduction

One of the most important areas of the law for a police officer to know is that of taking a suspected criminal into custody. The authority to deprive a person of his freedom carries with it a serious responsibility.

Any lack of understanding in this area of the law can subject an officer to serious consequences from false arrest suits and possible discharge from his job.

In this chapter we will examine the essential elements of the laws of arrest. This is not a detailed presentation of the subject but will serve to correct any misconception and also form a foundation for further study in other courses.

Objectives

Upon completing this chapter, you should be able to:

1. Explain the basic conditions under which both a police officer and a private citizen may make an arrest, the manner in which an arrest is made, the amount of force authorized and the legal steps necessary immediately following an arrest

Lecture Notes Outline

I. Definition of arrest:

   A. Purpose of an arrest:

II. How an arrest is made:
   A. Notifications:

   B. Restraint:
     1. Physical:

     2. Constructive:

   C. Advising defendant of rights:

III. Peace officer's authority to arrest (836 PC):
   A. Arrests for past or future crimes:

   B. Felony arrest:
     1. Crime committed in presence:

     2. Reasonable cause:
       a. Defined

      a. Guilt or acquittal:

      b. "Reasonable cause" vs. "Suspicion":

   C. Misdemeanor arrest:

IV. Private person's arrest (837 PC):
   A. Citizenship:

   B. Age:

   C. Authority:
     1. Misdemeanor:

     2. Felony:

V. Use of force:
   A. Basic Rules:

B. Purposes or objectives for using force:
    1. Arrest (835 PC):

    2. Defense (692 PC):

    3. Punishment (not valid):

C. Amount of force:
    1. Dangerous felony:

    2. Non-dangerous felony or misdemeanor:

D. Dilemma in use of force:

E. Consideration in the use of force by an officer:

    1.

    2.

    3.

F. Frequency of police shootings:

VI. Arrests on Private Property:

VII. Detaining for investigation:

    A. Length of detention:

    B. Comparison to Authority to Arrest:

Reading Assignment

1. California Penal Code Sections: 834, 835, 836, 837, 841 & 844
2. Black, Henry C., *Black's Law Dictionary,* West Publishing Co., St. Paul, Minn., 1951: Definition of "arrest."

Definitions

Define or explain the following:
A. arrest:

B. reasonable cause:

C. investigative detention:

1. What is the basic difference between a peace officer's authority to make an arrest for a felony and for a misdemeanor?

2. While on patrol in a police radio car at 2 A.M. you observe a man climbing through the rear window of a house. You tell him to halt and question him. He refuses to give any explanation for his actions or to identify himself other than to claim that it is his house. There is no one in the house or adjacent buildings. You arrest him and take him to the station. At the station it is proven that he was telling the truth; it was his house and he was going through the window because he had been locked out. He had refused to identify himself because he didn't like the manner in which you shouted at him. He is released and later sues you for false arrest. What will be the outcome?

3. You observe a man remove a case of motor oil from a loading dock. When he sees you, he drops the case and runs. You shout to him that he is under arrest for petty theft. He is a faster runner that you and is getting away. What do you do to stop him?

4. You receive a radio call of a fight. When you arrive at the location the fight is over. One man has a bloody nose and claims that the other hit him. Several witnesses agree with his story and say that the fighter should be taken to jail. What will you do?

5. A suspect is arrested without being advised of any of his "Miranda Decision" rights. Does this fact invalidate the arrest? Explain your answer.

Use of Force Continuum

Every law enforcement agency will have a use of force policy which will include a Use of Force Continuum. Officers will be first introduced to a use of force continuum during their academy training. While the individual agency's policies and continuums may have some minor variations they follow the same basic principles.

The following information is not intended to replace, or even supplement, what you might receive during your academy training or as part of any agency's use of force policy. It is solely intended to give you a general idea of how a Use of Force Continuum might be presented.

We must first identify a classification of subjects which officers will encounter:

Passive Compliant: A subject who follows the officer's request or verbal directions.

Passive Resistor: A subject who does not follow the officer's request or verbal directions but offers no physical resistance to the officer's attempt to gain control (e.g., someone who just goes limp).

Active Resistor: A subject who does not follow the officer's request or verbal directions, offers physical resistance that attempts to prevent the officer from gaining control, but does not attempt to harm the officer (e.g., bracing or pulling away, attempting to flee).

Active Aggressor: A subject who attempts to harm or attack the officer.

Use of Force Levels:

Level 1- Officer Presence: Officer Presence refers to the officer's appearance, demeanor, verbal and non-verbal communications that create an atmosphere of compliance.

Level 2 – Verbal Commands: Verbal commands are given in the form of task direction with consequences aimed at the subject.

Level 3 – Control Techniques: Control techniques are techniques or actions that have a low probability of causing connective tissue damage, lacerations of the skin or broken bones (these include pain-compliance, joint manipulation and escort techniques).

Level 4 – Aggressive Response Techniques: Aggressive response techniques are techniques or actions with a probability of causing connective tissue damage, lacerations to the skin, or broken bones, or that will cause irritation of the skin, eyes and/or mucous membranes (these include punches, kicks, strikes, takedowns and pepper spray).

Level 5 – Intermediate Weapons: Intermediate weapons are techniques or actions with a high probability of causing connective tissue damage, lacerations of the skin or broken bones (they include the use of the baton, taser guns, "bean bag," and other "less than lethal" munitions).

Level 6 – Deadly Force: Deadly Force is any force that is likely to cause serious physical injury or death.

While the situation will dictate what level is the most appropriate, an officer always wants to start at the lowest level possible and then adjust up or down as necessary. Levels 1, 2 and 3 are appropriate for the passive compliant and passive resistor while levels 4, 5 or 6 might be necessary with an active resistor or active aggressor.

Chapter 7

Fundamental Concepts of Judicial Procedure

Introduction

Most of the fundamental concepts of American justice were adopted from the English common law, a system founded on principals of fairness and honesty. Most people have a vague understanding that doctrines such as "presumption of innocence" and "trial by jury" exist but have little realization of their impact on daily courtroom proceedings in criminal trials. The guarantees established by these doctrines do not exist in some countries where the police, prosecutors and courts serve to keep a totalitarian government in power. In a free society, the police exist to serve and protect rather than to dominate. Thus, they must understand and support the underlying principles of the common law which guarantee a fair and impartial trial to a defendant.

Objectives

Upon completion of this chapter you should be able to:

1. Describe the following basic concepts of English common law and American judicial procedure:
    a. The doctrine of presumption of innocence.
    b. The degree of proof necessary for conviction in a criminal case compared to a civil case.
    c. The difference in responsibilities of the judge and the jury.

FUNDAMENTAL CONCEPTS OF JUDICIAL PROCEDURE

A programmed lesson for Self-Instruction

This chapter will be presented through the use of another programmed lesson similar to the ones used previously. Answer questions in the program as you work through the chapter.

Once again, you should follow the directions carefully and if you experience difficulty go back and reread the instructions for Chapter 1.

Start Here

1. We have already given some attention in previous chapters to the most basic rule of English common law: the presumption of innocence. Under our form of jurisprudence, the defendant is considered innocent of any crime until he is proven guilty. The burden is on the prosecutor to establish the evidence and prove that the defendant is guilty. This is not necessarily true in every country of the world. There are some legal systems in which an arrest or accusation by the police and prosecutor is sufficient to raise the conclusion that the suspect is guilty as charged and he must prove his innocence. Most countries believe in "innocent until proven guilty," however. Turn to paragraph 5.
2. Good, you're right.   Go on to paragraph 3.

3. The prosecutor is a criminal case proves the corpus delicti of a crime and establishes a simple prima facie case against the defendant. The defendant, acting as his own attorney, refuses to take the witness stand or produce any evidence in his own behalf. If the case is presented to the jury at this point, which side should win?
 	
    If your answer is the defense, turn to paragraph 12.
    If your answer is the prosecutor, turn to paragraph 17.

4. No, you missed that one too.
 	
    The prosecutor should win at this point because he has established reasonable proof of the defendant's guilt. It's now up to the defendant to present evidence of his innocence.
 	
    Before we go on to the next concept in this chapter, it might be wise for you to turn back to Chapter 3 where we first discussed prima facie cases and read paragraph 36. Then come back to this chapter and start again at paragraph 16. Follow on with the instructions from there and see how you make out.
    If you still have difficulty understand this concept, ask your instructor to help you.

5. True or False?
 	
    The presumption of innocence is exclusively an American legal concept.
 	
    If the above statement is true, turn to paragraph 10.   (Don't forget to circle the
    If the above statement is false, turn to paragraph 15.   answer on the answer sheet)

6. No, Sorry, you missed that one. It is up to the defendant to offer proof of what he is claiming as a defense. The prosecutor bears the burden of proving overall guilt in a criminal case, but he is not required to disprove the defendant's claims to various defenses. Presenting evidence of a claimed defense is up to the defendant.   Go on to paragraph 7.

7. The prosecutor in a criminal case proves the corpus delicti of a crime and establishes a simple prima facie case against the defendant. The defendant, acting as his own attorney, refuses to take the witness stand or produce any evidence in his own behalf. If the case is presented to the jury at this point, which side should win?

     If your answer is the defense, turn to paragraph 4.
     If your answer is the prosecutor, turn to paragraph 13.

8. The term "preponderance of the evidence" means _Majority or 51%_ of the evidence.

   Write in you answer and turn to paragraph 14.

9. In determining whether a preponderance of the evidence has been presented, which is of more value: the total amount of evidence presented by each side or the quality of the evidence presented?

     If your answer is amount, turn to paragraph 22.
     If your answer is quality, turn to paragraph 18.

10. Sorry, you're wrong. The presumption of innocence is a prominent part of American judicial procedure but it is not ours alone. It did not even originate here in the United States. England established the doctrine as a procedural rule of low long before we were a nation. It still exists in England and many other countries today.

     Please turn to paragraph 16.

11. A defendant charged with murder claims that he killed the victim is self-defense when the victim was about to attack him. Which side in the case must prove whether the victim was actually attacking or not and whether self-defense is a valid claim?

     If your answer is the defense, turn to paragraph 2.   (Make sure you answer on
     If your answer is the prosecutor, turn to paragraph 6.   the answer sheet also.)

12. Too bad; you missed that one. Remember back in Chapter 3 when we discussed prima facie cases and the burden of proof? If the prosecution has established a satisfactory prima facie case and the defendant offers nothing to contradict it, then the prosecution should win because the presumption of innocence has been overcome. Don't forget that a prima facie case means there is reasonable evidence to believe that the defendant is guilty. The defendant must then offer evidence of his innocence.

     You're still doing all right so go on to paragraph 21.

13. Good! You're right on that one. You're getting back on track again. The prosecutor should win because a prima facie case means there is reasonable proof of the defendant's guilt. It then becomes the defendant's responsibility to offer evidence of his innocence.

     Go on to paragraph 21.

14. Your answer should have been either: a majority or 51%

If you answered correctly, turn to paragraph 9.
If you gave any other answer, turn to paragraph 24.

15. Right. The presumption of innocence is a prominent part of American judicial procedure but it isn't ours exclusively. Many other countries abide by the same standard.

Go on to paragraph 16.

16. Although the fundamental burden of proof is on the prosecution in a criminal case, this does not mean that the defense is never required to offer proof of facts in question. Once the prosecutor has established a prima facie case against the defendant, it is expected that the defense will then provide evidence of innocence. In doing so, the defendant then has the burden of proving the truth and validity of any defense which he is claiming.

Turn to paragraph 11.

17. Good, you're right again.

Go right on to paragraph 21.

18. Good, that's two right answers in a row.

Keep right on moving to paragraph 34.

19. No, it's not. The standard, or degree of proof known as "the preponderance of the evidence," applies to civil cases only. Criminal cases use the "guilt beyond a reasonable doubt" standard.

Go on to paragraph 30 but be sure to read carefully.

20. Now hold it a minute. You're getting cocky because you got the last question right. You missed this one. "Proof beyond a reasonable doubt" means more or better evidence than just a "preponderance of the evidence," the standard used in civil cases. Think it over. Remember that in a civil case 51% of the evidence must favor the winning side but that in a criminal case, the prosecutor must have 70, 80 or 90 % in order to convict the defendant.

Go on to paragraph 31 but be careful.

21. Let's go on to a new idea now: the degree of proof. This refers to the amount of proof necessary for one side or the other to win the case in court.

In a civil case, the degree of proof necessary to win the case is known as "a preponderance of the evidence." This simply means that a majority of the evidence presented must favor the winning side. If 51% of the evidence in a civil case points toward the plaintiff as being right then he should win the case. If 51% points the other way, then the defendant should win.

(continue on to the next page)

The phrase "preponderance of the evidence" and these percentage figures don't just refer to the quantity of the evidence. They really mean the quality and credibility of the evidence. If one side produces seven witnesses and the opposite party presents only three witnesses, the one with seven doesn't win on volume alone. The jury still has to evaluate the overall effect and value of the testimony in order to determine which side has presented a "preponderance of the evidence."

Turn to paragraph 8.

---

22. Now hold on! You got the last question right. How come you missed on this one? It's not amount or quantity of evidence that's important in a case, it's the quality of the evidence … the validity.

Go back to paragraph 21 and read the last part of it, then come back here.

See? It's not the quantity; it's the quality that counts.

If you're ready now, let's go on to paragraph 34.

---

23. Right. That's two in a row on this part of the program.

Go right on to paragraph 28.

---

24. In determining whether a preponderance of the evidence has been presented, which is of more value: the total amount of the evidence presented by each side or the quality of the evidence presented?

If your answer is amount, turn to paragraph 29.
If your answer is quality, turn to paragraph 33.

---

25. True or False?

The preponderance of evidence standard is applied equally to both civil and criminal cases.

If your answer is true, turn to paragraph 19.
If your answer is false, turn to paragraph 35.

---

26. No. Hold it a moment. You did so well on the last question you got cocky. "Proof beyond a reasonable doubt" means more or better evidence than just "preponderance of the evidence," the standard used in civil cases. Think it over. Remember that in a civil case 51% of the evidence must favor the winning side but that in a criminal case the prosecutor must have 70, 80 or 90% in order to convict the defendant.

Go on to paragraph 31 but be careful.

---

27. That's better. You got that one right. The amount of proof needed in a criminal case is greater than the amount needed in civil cases. Just keep reading the questions carefully and think about them before you answer.

Go on to paragraph 42.

28. Is the following statement true or false?

   The jury is a criminal case must be absolutely convinced of the defendant's guilt and if there appears to be any possibility of his innocence he should be acquitted.

   If your answer is true, turn to paragraph 38.
   If your answer is false, turn to paragraph 32.

29. Now hold everything! That's two wrong in a row. I think you may be reading things too fast and not fully understanding them.

   Go back to paragraph 21 and continue on from there.

30. In a criminal case, the degree of proof necessary to convict a defendant is known as proof beyond a reasonable doubt. This degree of proof is:

   1. Less than what is necessary for a civil case.
   2. The same as for a civil case.
   3. More than required for a civil case.

   If your answer is 1, turn to paragraph 37.
   If your answer is 2, turn to paragraph 41.
   If your answer is 3, turn to paragraph 27.

31. Is the following statement true or false?

   The jury in a criminal case must be absolutely convinced of the defendant's guilt and if there appears to be any possibility of his innocence he should be acquitted.

   If your answer it true, turn to paragraph 43.
   If you answer is false, turn to paragraph 39.

32. Excellent, you're still getting them right.

   In considering reasonable doubt, remember that the judgment of man is not perfect. Neither is his recollection of events or his ability to secure evidence of truth. In his attempt to determine truth he will be subject to error. In the creation of our legal system, every effort has been made to avoid the unjust conviction of an innocent person. But we cannot demand absolute perfection in the system. We cannot require freedom from all possibility of error. To do so would be to demand the impossible. Our standard of "reasonable doubt" has proven itself over many years in thousands of cases. It is probably as close to perfection as we can achieve. To demand greater proof would defeat the ends of justice.

   Go on to paragraph 47.

33. O.K. Now you're getting back with it. It is quality of the evidence that's important, not total amount.

Try to keep getting the right answers. Read the material carefully so that you're sure that you understand it before answering the questions.

Go on to paragraph 34.

34. What we've discussed about the degree of proof thus far – the preponderance of evidence concept – refers to civil cases only, not criminal. A different standard of proof is required in criminal cases. A criminal defendant must be found guilty "beyond a reasonable doubt" in order for him to be convicted. This is a greater degree of proof than the preponderance of the evidence required in civil cases.

Under the "preponderance of the evidence" standard used in civil cases it was relatively simple to establish 51% as a guideline figure in determining whether the standard had been achieved. In determining what amount of evidence establishes guilt "beyond a reasonable doubt," no simple percentage figure can be used. It would mean beyond 51% in every case, but whether it would require 70, 80 or 90% in a specific case, no one can say.

Finding a defendant guilty beyond a reasonable doubt means that the jury is morally convinced of his guilt and they feel no pangs of conscience in convicting hem. It does not mean that they must feel convinced beyond all possible doubt. Everything dealing with the proof of human acts and behavior may be open to some doubt.

This differing standard of proof in civil and criminal cases is one of the reasons why the same case, against the same defendant, with the same evidence, tried first in criminal court and then in a civil court may have different verdicts. In the civil case the amount of evidence might be sufficient to find him guilty yet not be enough to prove guilt "beyond a reasonable doubt" for the criminal case.

Turn to paragraph 25.

35. Right again!

Go right on to paragraph 36.

36. In a criminal case, the degree of proof necessary to convict a defendant is known as proof beyond a reasonable doubt. This degree of proof is:

1. Less than what is necessary for a civil case.
2. The same as for a civil case.
3. More than required for a civil case.

If your answer is 1, turn to paragraph 26.
If your answer is 2, turn to paragraph 20.
If your answer is 3, turn to paragraph 23.

37. Now hold it a minute. That's two wrong in a row

How about taking a little review?

Turn to paragraph 46

38. Slow down. You're getting in trouble. You were doing great up to now, but let's look at that last answer again. Is it really true that a jury must be absolutely convinced of the defendant's guilt?

Go back to paragraph 28 and pick another answer.

39. Right. It's not necessary that the jury be absolutely convinced of the defendant's guilt.

To be certain that you understand this important rule …

Turn now to paragraph 48.

40. Is the following statement true or false?

The jury in a criminal case must be absolutely convinced of the defendant's guilt and if there appears to be the slightest possibility of his innocence he should be acquitted.

If your answer is true, turn to paragraph 44.
If your answer is false, turn to paragraph 45.

41. Now hold it a minute. That's two wrong in a row. How about taking a little review?

Turn to paragraph 46.

42. Is the following statement true or false?

The jury in a criminal case must be absolutely convinced of the defendant's guilt and if there appears to be any possibility of his innocence he should be acquitted.

If your answer is true, turn to paragraph 43.
If your answer is false, turn to paragraph 39.

43. Slow down. You're getting in trouble again. We said that a jury must find the defendant guilty "beyond a *reasonable* doubt." That word "reasonable" is most important. It doesn't mean that the jury must not have any possible doubt. After all the evidence has been weighed and evaluated the jury may still feel that there is a small possibility that the defendant is innocent. But if that possibility is so small that it cannot really be considered a reasonable possibility, then the defendant should be convicted. Remember that the judgment of man is not perfect. In his attempt to determine truth he will be subjected to error. In the creation of our legal system, every effort has been made to avoid the unjust conviction of an innocent person. But we cannot demand absolute perfection in the system. We cannot require freedom from all possibility of error. To do so would be to demand the impossible. Our standard of "reasonable doubt" has proven itself over many years in thousands of cases. It is probably as close to perfection as we can achieve. To demand greater proof would defeat the ends of justice.

Go on to paragraph 47.

44. No, I'm sorry, you missed again. I think you'd better take a full review.

   Go back to paragraph 34 and continue on from there.

45. Right. It's not necessary that the jury be absolutely convinced of the defendant's guilt. It looks like you're getting back on the track again but to be certain that you understand this important rule …

   Turn now to paragraph 48

46. Now first of all, remember to keep criminal and civil cases separate in you mind when thinking about standards of proof. Different sets of rules apply to each. In a civil case we only need a preponderance of the evidence (over 50%) for one side or the other to win. In a criminal case the prosecution has the burden of going further than that. They must show that the defendant is guilty "beyond a reasonable doubt," which means more proof than the 51% required in a civil case.

   Turn to paragraph 40 but read it carefully and think of your answer.

47. In the final portion of this lesson we will examine the different duties imposed upon the judge and jury. Each has certain defined responsibilities in determining the outcome of a case. Seldom does one invade the domain of the other.

   First, let's look at the work of the judge. He or she has three basic tasks to perform during the trial:
   1. First, to decide questions of law and court procedure. This is probably his or her most important task. For example, if there is disagreement between the attorneys concerning the definition of burglary, the judge must rule on the true meaning and interpretation of the law. It is also the judge's responsibility to determine the form and sequence which the trial will follow. The judge must also decide whether challenged evidence is admissible in the trial or should be excluded from consideration.

   2. The second function of the judge is similar to the first but casts him or her more in the role of a teacher. After the evidence has been presented to the jury and they have heard the last witness and examined the last exhibit, the jury must then be instructed concerning the law which they must apply to the case. The opposing attorneys submit proposed jury instructions to the judge. If acceptable, the judge present them to the jury in the form of written and verbal instructions.

   3. The final responsibility of the judge is to determine the defendant's sentence if the jury returns a guilty verdict. There are a few exceptions to this, but in most cases, this decision is strictly the province of the judge. It is here that he or she must exercise more than simply knowledge of logic; their deepest beliefs and emotions will affect this decision. This is the most difficult task and the one in which there will be the greatest variation between judges. This is where they truly become a "judge"; manipulating and controlling the destiny of the person before them.

These, then, are the three basic functions of the judge.

   Turn to paragraph 52.

48. Finding the defendant guilty "beyond a reasonable doubt" doesn't mean that the jury must not have any doubt. After all the evidence has been examined and weighed the jury may still feel that there is a small possibility that the defendant is innocent. But it that possibility is so small that it cannot really be considered a reasonable possibility, then the defendant should be convicted. Remember that the judgment of man is not perfect. Neither is his recollection of events or his ability to secure evidence of truth. In his attempt to determine truth he will be subject to error. In the creation of our legal system every effort has been made to avoid the unjust conviction of an innocent person. But we cannot demand absolute perfection in the system. We cannot require freedom from all possibility of error. To do so would be to demand the impossible. Our standard of "reasonable doubt" has proven itself over many years in thousands of cases. It is probably as close to perfection as we can achieve. To demand greater proof would defeat the ends of justice.

Go on to paragraph 47.

49. Right. The jury seldom becomes involved in deciding the sentence which a defendant will receive. This is almost always left to the judge.

Continue on to paragraph 50.

50. In the following spaces, list the three primary tasks of the judge in a criminal case:

1. _____.

2. _____,

3. _____.

Turn to paragraph 53.

51. In the following spaces, list the three primary tasks of the jury in a criminal case:

1. _____.

2. _____.

3. _____.

Turn to paragraph 54.

52. True or False?

In most criminal cases the jury is called upon to sentence a convicted defendant. This is usually the most difficult decision which the jury is required to make.

> If your answer it true, turn to paragraph 56.
> If your answer is false, turn to paragraph 49.

53. The correct answers are:

1. Decide question of law and court procedure.
2. Instruct the jury in the law which they should apply to the case.
3. Decide on the sentence that a guilty defendant will receive.

> If you got all three right, continue to paragraph 57.
> If you missed two or more, return to paragraph 47 and continue from there.
> If you only missed one, decide for yourself whether you understand the material or should go back to paragraph 47 and review. Just remember, you're going to be tested on it some day soon

54. The correct answers are:

1. Decide on the truthfulness and accuracy of witnesses.
2. Determine the facts of what actually occurred.
3. Decide on the defendant's guilt or innocence.

> If you missed any one of these, return to paragraph 57 to review.
> If you were right on all three, go to paragraph 55.

55. Just a few final points now and that will be all.

There are some trials in which both sides agree not to have a jury. This type of trial is called a "court trial" Or "trial by court." In this case the judge performs the functions of both judge and jury. There are also proceeding called "law and motion" hearings in which there is no jury. This happens when the case consists of legal disagreements only and there is no argument about the facts of the case. In that case there is nothing for a jury to decide and so none is used. The case is heard only by the judge.

Turn to paragraph 59.

56. Maybe you misread the question. Or perhaps you just don't like true and false questions. In any event, you got it wrong. It is true that when the jury is required to pass sentence on a defendant, it can be a very difficult task. But the jury very rarely is obliged to perform this duty. It is almost always the responsibility of the judge.

Turn now to paragraph 50.

57. Now let's look at the work of the jury. They also have three distinct jobs.

    1. First, they must decide on the truthfulness and accuracy of witnesses. Our entire legal system is built on the assumption that witnesses will testify truthfully. They take an oath to this effect and can be punished for the crime of perjury if they deliberately lie. But in spite of this, there is a substantial amount of deception which takes place in our law courts. Witnesses will swear that they were present when you arrested the defendant and clearly observed that he was sober and in complete control of himself when you know that he had forced three lanes of traffic to a halt and fell out of his car when you stopped him. But it is up to the jury to unsnarl this tangled web of fabrication. Sometimes they will believe you, sometimes the other side.

    2. The second job of the jury evolves from the first. After listening to all the witnesses, examining all of the evidence and separating truth from fiction they must then determine the facts of what actually happened. Did the defendant break into a drugstore at 2 o'clock on a particular morning? If not, then what exactly did occur? This is their primary function – the determination of facts

    3. After these first two tasks are accomplished they must then decide guilt or innocence based on the facts, which they have established, and the instructions of law given to them by the judge. If the facts, as they see them, satisfy all of the elements of a crime as explained by the judge, then they should find the defendant guilty. If not, then they should acquit him.

    These then are the three major functions of the jury.

Turn to paragraph 51.

58. This is the end of the programmed lesson. Go on to the program study notes at the end of the chapter.

59. Remember that the kinds of proceedings, which do not use juries, are called court trials and law and motion hearings.

Go on to paragraph 58.

Program Study Notes

For study purposes, the paragraphs in this programmed lesson may be read in the following order:

1

16

21

34

32

47

57

55

    Following this order will allow you to skip the paragraphs which merely provide directions and will permit you to read only the paragraphs containing factual information

    Do *NOT* follow this outline for your initial study of the lesson. It is very important that you proceed according to directions the first time through in order to achieve the full benefit from programmed learning methods.

    Remember; don't use this outline until you have first completed the lesson in the manner directed by the instructions.

Definitions

Define or explain the following:

A. burden of proof:

B. presumption of innocence:

C. court trial:

D. jury trial:

E. reasonable doubt:

Reading Assignment

1. Penal Code Sections: 1044, 1096 & 1124 – 1127

Chapter Problems

1. A detective spends several weeks investigating a case before arresting the suspect. At the trial it appears that the evidence is about 60% against the suspect and about 40% in his favor. It is a nonjury trial and the judge acquits the suspect. Later, the judge tells the detective that he thought the defendant was probably guilty. The detective argues that he should have convicted the defendant if he thought he was probably guilty. How can the judge explain this decision to the detective?

2. If a case is tried first in criminal court and then in civil court, with exactly the same evidence, but has two different results, what is a probable reason?

3. I have been arrested for failing to pay my taxes. I admit that I did not file a tax return and do not challenge the accuracy of the facts. Instead, I argue that the tax laws are unconstitutional, and therefore, I cannot be punished. If I follow the proper procedures for this type of argument, will I receive a jury trial? Explain your answer fully.

Answer the following with either "judge" or "jury":

4. The facts of a case are decided by the _____.

5. The truthfulness of witnesses is decided by the _____.

6. The law of the case is decided by the _____.

7. Guilt or innocence of the defendant is decided by the _____.

8. The sentence is decided by the _____.

Chapter 8

Defenses to Crimes

Introduction

There are circumstances under which a defendant may cause injury or damage to another but not be guilty of a crime. For example, where the defendant's actions do not satisfy the requirements (corpus delicti) of a particular crime or where the defendant did not have a criminal intent. Other reasons may also exist under which a person may be excused for an act, which would otherwise be considered a crime. These various reasons for relieving a defendant of legal responsibility are called defenses.

An understanding of legal defenses is important to a law enforcement officer. In the investigation of a crime, an officer must anticipate the possible defenses which may be claimed by a defendant and gather all available evidence, which would tend to prove or disprove such claims. Much of this evidence is only available during the initial stages of the investigation, so possible defenses must be recognized and evidence gathered immediately.

In the collection and evaluation of evidence, an officer should keep in mind the basic functions of an investigator: to gather all available evidence of criminal activity and of potential defenses. If the evidence clearly indicates that the defendant has a valid defense, then the investigation and prosecution should be terminated. On the other hand, if the evidence of a defense is inconclusive or is contradicted by other evidence, then the case should be presented to a judge and jury for their determination of guilt or innocence.

In this chapter, we will examine the most common defenses, which may be claimed by a defendant. Later, in other chapters, you will review some of these defenses as they apply to specific crimes.

Objectives

Upon completing this chapter, you should be able to:

1. Explain the legal requirements of each of the following criminal defenses:
    insanity
    diminished capacity
    idiocy and feeble mindedness
    mistakes of law and fact
    double jeopardy
    unavoidable accidents
    entrapment
    duress and coercion
    self-defense
    statute of limitations

2. Given the facts of a criminal case, determine the most likely defenses which may be claimed and the evidence required to prove or disprove the validity of those defenses.

Lecture Notes Outline

I. General:
  A. Statutory defenses:

  1. Act and Intent:

  2. Procedural Defenses:

  B. Proof of defense:

  1. Burden of proof is on: _____.
  2. Multiple defenses:

II. Minors (26 PC):

III. Feeble mindedness (26 PC):

  A. Rules of legal responsibility:
  1. Mentally normal:

2. Mental age of 3 – 12: (Mentally impaired/challenged)

3. Mental age of under 3: (Severely mentally impaired/challenged)

IV. Insanity (26 PC):
  A. General:
    1. Definition:

    2. Theory and Difficulties:

    3. Distinguished from feeble mindedness:

  B. M'Naughten rule:
    1. History:

    2. Test:

      a.

b.

C. American Law Institute Rule:
    1. History:

    2. Rule:

    3. Difference between A.L.I. and M'Naughten rules:

D. Temporary insanity:

E. Cause of Insanity:

    1. Addiction and alcoholism: (25.5 PC)

F. Irresistible impulse:
   1. Defined:

G. Insanity defense trial procedures (1016 – 1026.6 PC):
   1. Burden of proof:

   2. Dual plea:

   3. Examination (1027PC):

   4. Dual trial:

      a.

      b.

   5. Time of insanity:

H. Result:
   1. Sane:

   2. Insane:

I. Diminished capacity (25 PC): *(Twinkie Defense)*

V. Mistake (26 PC):
  A. Mistake of law:

      1. Exception:

  B. Mistake of fact:
     1. When accepted as a defense:

     2. Exceptions:
         a. Negligence:

         b. Other crime intended:

VI. Unconscious acts (26 PC):

A. Examples:

VII. Misfortune and accident (26 PC):

VIII. Duress and coercion (26 PC):
    A. Definitions:
      1. Duress:

      2. Coercion:

    B. Factors affecting validity:

    C. Exclusion:

IX. Consent of victim:
    A. General:

    B. Exception:
        Consent of the victim may be a defense if _____

        _____ .

        1. Examples:

           a.

           b.

           c.

    C. Types of consent:
        1. Implied consent:

        2. Specific consent:

    D. Validity of consent:

X. Entrapment:
    A. Definition:

    B. Test:

C. Creating opportunity:

D. Examples:

E. Effect of entrapment:

F. Double jeopardy (687 PC):
1. Definition:

2. Exceptions:

a.

b.

c.

d.

e.

G. Use of Force in Arrest or Self Defense (692 – 694, 835 & 197 PC):
   1. General concepts:

   2. Legal requirements for use of force:

      a.

      b.

      c.

   3. Legal objectives or reasons for use of force:

      a.

      b.

      c. Other authorized objectives:

      d. Unlawful objectives:

   4. Reasonableness of amount of force:

      a. Two part test:
         (1) Subjective:

         (2) Objective:

5. Killing another in self defense (Justifiable homicide) (197 PC):
   a. Preventing a dangerous felony:

      (1) Dangerous felony defined:

   b. Misdemeanor and non-dangerous felonies:

   c. Lack of immediate danger:
      (1) Self-Defense:

      (2) Arrest:

6. Reasonable appearances:

7. Home protection:
   a. General Rule:

   b. Home Protection Rule (198.5 PC):

8. Danger created by party claiming self-defense (197(3) PC):

XI. Statute of limitations (799 – 803 PC):
    A. Definition:

    B. Time limits:
       1. Felonies:

       2. Felonies with sentences of 8 years or more: *(Mostly violent sex crimes.)*

       3. Misdemeanors and infractions:

       4. No limitation on:

          a.

          b.

          c.

       5. Optional crimes (805 PC):

    C. How calculated:

       1. Variations:

D. Effect of arrest an warrant:

E. Tolling the statute:

Reading Assignment

A. California Penal Code Sections: 26, 1026, 1027, 687, 692, 693, 694, 799 – 803

Definitions

Define or explain the following:
A. Feeblemindedness:

B. insanity:

C. M'Naughten rule:

D. irresistible impulse:

E. A.L.I. rule:

F. mistake of law:

G. mistake of fact:

H. unconscious acts:

I. duress and coercion:

J. entrapment:

K. double jeopardy:

L. statute of limitations:

N. tolling the statute:

Chapter Problems

1. D. Haynes is arrested while participating in a burglary. As his defense he claims that two older friends talked him into participating and that he otherwise would not have participated in the burglary. The judge accepts this defense and dismisses the charges against the defendant. The District Attorney argues that the dismissal is improper. If the District Attorney files an appeal with the appellate court, what should be the outcome? Why?

2. John and Mary were having a beach party with their friends Joe and Phyliss. Joe and John playfully wrestle in the sand while Mary and Phyliss prepare the lunch they have brought. The friendly wrestling match ends with John sitting on Joe's chest. Joe gets irritated and tells John to get off. John laughs and tells Mary to pour some sand on Joe's face. Mary declines because she can see that Joe is getting angry. John insists and finally orders Mary to pour the sand on Joe. Mary starts to pour the sand over Joe when Phyliss, in an attempt to prevent Joe from being further injured, pushes John from behind. John falls over and dislocates his shoulder when he lands on the sand. Joe immediately jumps up and proceeds to kick John severely about the head for several minutes until he is finally stopped by lifeguards who are called by Mary and Phyliss. Give the possible criminal charges against all parties, the probable defenses that they will claim to these charges and indicate what the final results will probably be. Explain in detail.

3. Pete Patroni is standing on the observation platform of the Empire State Building when a sudden gust of wind knocks him off balance and he falls against his mother-in-law who is pushed over the edge. Pete enters two defenses: accident and insanity. He proves that the incident was a complete accident and that he was not negligent in any manner but he fails to prove that he was insane. Assuming that New York law is the same as California will Pete be found Guilty? Explain you answer.

4. Fred Fruitcake, 23 year old inmate of Norwalk Mental Hospital, escapes from the hospital and hits you in the face because you remind him o f one of his nurses whom he dislikes. Fred has a mental age of about 2 ½. Can he be convicted of any crime? How can you be repaid for your medical bills for the broken nose?

5. Pete Pathetic is driving home at 3 A.M. and stops by his local gas station to pick up a tire that he had left for repairs. The station is closed but he finds a tire, which he believes, is his and puts in his trunk. He is about to leave when he notices a wallet on the floor of the phone booth at the station. He glances at the operator's license in the wallet, takes the money from it, and then places it next to the door of the station where it will be found by the station owner. The next morning he discovers that the tire is not his and returns it. His is later arrested and charged with petty theft for taking the tire and theft of lost property for taking the money from the wallet. He claims that he thought the tire was his and that he didn't think it was against the law to take money from a lost wallet. What will be the result on both counts? Explain your answer.

6. Sue is a kleptomaniac. She is arrested for stealing from a department store and claims insanity as her defense. The shock of being arrested and placed in jail causes a mental breakdown and when she appears for trial she is unable to comprehend what is going on in court. What procedural steps will be taken and what will probably be the final outcome of the case?

Chapter 9

Attempts to Commit Crimes

Introduction

The law is reasonably clear in describing what facts must exist in order to establish that a crime has occurred. There must be evidence to prove that all the elements of the particular crime have been satisfied. If not, then no crime has actually occurred and therefore no one can be convicted of having committed the crime.

But what if a person tries to commit a crime, but does not succeed? Under early common law, he was simply considered to be innocent of any wrongdoing, and could not be punished because he had not satisfied all the elements of the intended crime.

However, such a person could still be a threat to others if he is allowed to keep trying. What can be done to prevent him from continuing in his efforts and perhaps succeeding at a later date?

The answer is that the act of trying to commit a crime is a crime all by itself. We call this an "Attempted Crime", and it is prohibited by California Penal Code Sections 21a and 664.

Through the legal mechanism of prohibiting the attempt to commit a crime, we may take action to arrest and prosecute the person who tries by fails, and thereby prevent them from continuing to be a threat to the victim.

Objectives

Upon completing this chapter, you should be able to:

1. Describe the elements of an attempted crime (21a PC).
2. Describe the circumstances under which a legal or factual impossibility to complete the crime may prevent an act from being an attempted crime.
3. Describe the legal status of a person who intends to commit a crime, initiates actions to carry it out, but then voluntarily abandons his efforts without completing the crime.
4. Describe the penalties for an attempted crime (664 PC)>

Note:

This subject may be taught in either the Concepts of Criminal Law class or the Substantive Criminal Law class, depending on the preferences of the individual college or police academy. In this workbook, it is included as part of the material for the Concepts of Criminal Law course.

Rather than using the note taking outline format used in previous chapters, this chapter is written in the form of a study guide as opposed to a complete narrative text describing the subject of attempted crimes.

I. Corpus Delicti of an Attempted Crime (21a PC):

A criminal attempt under section 21a PC consists of a very simple corpus delicti. As you already know, the corpus delicti of every crime must consist of at least two elements: an action element and a mental, or intent element. An attempt crime includes just the bare minimum number of elements to satisfy this requirement:

A. An intent to commit a criminal act.

B. A direct, but ineffectual act toward committing the crime, which comes dangerously close to success.

II. Analysis of Elements:

A. The Intent element:

Attempting to commit a crime is a specific intent crime. The defendant must have deliberately intended to commit the crime that he is charged with attempting. A criminal attempt cannot occur through mere negligence or carelessness.

1. The following example may help to clarify this rule:

a. A defendant who kills someone while driving a car in a negligent manner is guilty of manslaughter, a general intent crime.

b. Assume that a defendant is speeding and driving recklessly as he approaches a pedestrian. If he hits and kills the pedestrian, he will be guilty of manslaughter.

c. But if the pedestrian is able to jump out of the path of the speeding car just in time to avoid being hit, is the driver guilty of attempted manslaughter?

(1) The answer is NO. In the crime of manslaughter, the defendant does not deliberately intend to commit a crime. Manslaughter occurs only through a defendant's negligence, not because of his deliberate, wrongful intentions.

(2) In order to be guilty of attempting to commit a crime, a defendant must act intentionally …. Negligence will not suffice. Therefore, a driver who almost hits a pedestrian through Negligence is not guilty of attempted manslaughter.

2. Because manslaughter is not an intentional crime, there is no such crime as attempted manslaughter.

B. Action element:

1. The act necessary to constitute an attempt must be something that comes "Dangerously close to success". That means that the defendant must go beyond mere preparation. The defendant's actions must be such that, in all likelihood, the intended crime would have been completed except for some outside intervening factor, such as being observed and forced to stop by someone else.

2. To be guilty of an attempt, the defendant must also go further than the type of "Overt" act required for a conspiracy. He must come dangerously close to success.

3. Whether the defendant has gone far enough to be considered "dangerously close to success" is a factual question for the jury to determine. The jury may consider the seriousness of the crime, closeness of the defendant to the victim or to the scene of the crime, tools or weapons in the defendant's possession which are to be used in committing the crime, the cause of the defendant's failure to complete the crime and other factors which indicate the likelihood of the defendant's success.

The following indicates the various degrees of proximity or closeness which must exist between The defendant's actions and a completed crime in order for the defendant in incur criminal liability.

a. Planning or thinking about committing a crime, with nothing more, will not impose an criminal responsibility.

b. An agreement, coupled with an overt act, may constitute the crime of conspiracy.

c. Intending to commit a crime and doing something which comes dangerously close to success may make a person guilty of an attempt.

d. Satisfying all of the elements of the intended crime will make a defendant criminally responsible for the completed crime.

III. Impossibility Problems:

One of the unique problems related to the crime of attempt is the question of the defendant's liability if he embarks on the commission of a crime but then finds that it is impossible for him to complete the intended crime.

There is considerable debate and confusion surrounding this area of the law, but the most common view is that these situations fall into two categories: those involving legal impossibilities, and those involving factual impossibilities. It is frequently difficult to distinguish between the two.

A. Legal impossibility:

1. A legal impossibility is a situation where, if the defendant successfully completed all of his intended actions, he still would not have satisfied the corpus delicti of the intended crime.

Let's look at two examples:

a. In the case of State vs. Guffey, 262 SW2 152, the defendant saw a deer standing by the side of the road in a wooded area. He took aim and fired at the deer even though he knew that it was out of hunting season and illegal to hunt deer on that particular date. After firing the shot he became aware that the animal he was shooting at was not a live animal at all, but was just a stuffed deer used as part of a roadside advertising sign. Unfortunately, he was observed by a state game warder, who cited him for hunting deer out of season. When the defendant pointed out that he could not be guilty of the violation because, after all, he wasn't actually shooting at a live deer, the warden then cited him for attempting to hunt deer out of season.

The court ruled that, because it is legally impossible to violate the hunting laws by shooting at a stuffed animal, it likewise does not constitute an attempt to violate the hunting laws. He was judged not guilty of either hunting out of season, or attempting to hunt out of season.

b. The same result was reached in the case of State vs. Taylor, 345 Mo. 325, when the defendant attempted to bribe a juror after, unknown to the defendant, the juror had already been released from jury duty. The defendant was found not guilty of attempted bribery because, even if the person had accepted, it would not have been bribery of a juror as the person was not, in fact, a member of the jury at the time of the bribe. Because it was a legal impossibility to complete the crime of bribery, it was also not an attempted bribery.

C. Factual Impossibility:

A factual impossibility is a situation where the defendant cannot complete the intended crime because of factors that exist, which prevents the completion of all the elements of the crime but where, otherwise, the corpus delicti could have been satisfied.

The general rule relating to factual impossibilities is that if the error was a reasonable mistake, and just a slight miscalculation of the facts, the defendant is still guilty of an attempted crime, if his actions come dangerously close to success.

Let's look at two examples of this rule.

a. In People vs. Fiegelman, 33 CA2 100, the defendant tried to pick an empty pocket. Obviously he got nothing because the pocket was empty. Nevertheless, he was still guilty of attempted theft.

b. In another case, a defendant, intending to kill someone, planted gunpowder in a stove in the victim's kitchen. The stove exploded and demolished the kitchen when the gunpowder was ignited prematurely by the heat of the pilot light in the stove. The victim was not there at the time and was not injured, but the defendant was still found guilty of attempted murder (People vs. Pape, 66 Cal. 366).

In the case of an unreasonable error in judgment, where there is little likelihood of success, the defendant is not held responsible.

Here are two interesting cases involving unreasonable errors in which the defendant was not guilty of an attempted crime because there was so little possibility that the crime could have succeeded in the manner chosen:

a. A defendant believed she could kill the victim by sticking pins in a voodoo doll. She was found not guilty of attempted murder.

b. In a second case, a defendant intended to kill the Mayor of San Francisco by planting a bomb under a park bench in Golden Gate Park. The bomb exploded at 2:00 AM, the time that it was set to go off. Later investigation showed that the Mayor never intended to be in the park at that time of night, and there was no reason whatever for anyone to believe that he would be sitting on that particular park bench at 2 in the morning. The defendant was found not guilty of attempted murder.

IV. Abandonment:

Once the elements of any crime have been satisfied, the crime is complete, regardless of subsequent events.

If a defendant, in attempting to commit a crime, has progressed far enough to satisfy the corpus delicti of an attempted crime, it is immaterial whether he voluntarily abandons his plan by his own decision or is forced to stop. The defendant is still guilty of an attempted crime.

Examples:

1. A defendant intends to shoot a victim with a rifle from some distance away. He has the intended victim lined up in his gun sight, ready to pull the trigger, but then is suddenly discovered and is prevented from firing the weapon when the gun is yanked out of his grasp.

   Is he guilty of attempted murder: -- YES. He has gone far enough to satisfy the elements of an attempted murder.

2. Suppose, in the same situation, the defendant has a change of heart, and, at the last moment, voluntarily abandons the idea of killing the victim. If he has already gone far enough to come close to success, is he guilty of attempted murder? The answer is – YES.

   No matter what happens, if the defendant has gone far enough to satisfy the elements of an attempted crime, that fact cannot be erased simply by the defendant deciding not to go further and complete the intended crime. The elements of an attempted crime have been satisfied and the defendant may still be prosecuted for that.

V. Penalties for attempting to commit a crime (664 PC):

Finally, let's look at the penalties for attempting to commit a crime. Generally, an attempted crime can carry up to one half of the sentence for the completed crime.

Where the intended crime carries a possible life or death sentence, an attempt carries a sentence of 5, 7 or 9 years.

Reading Assignment

1. Penal Code Sections 21a, 663, 664 & 665.

Definitions

Define the following:

A. Ineffectual

Chapter Problem

1. Sam Spivel intends to kill his employer, Carl Cubit. He knows that Carl is excitable and has a heart condition so he intends to frighten him in hopes of bringing on a heart attack. Sam carries out his plan by starting an argument with Carl and waving an unloaded gun at him. Sam knows that the gun is unloaded and cannot fire. As predicted, Carl has a heart attack but recovers. Can Sam be convicted of attempted murder? Explain your answer.

2. Two soldiers want to scare a friend who is afraid of snakes. They put two harmless snakes on his chest while he is asleep and then start to wake him up. Their sergeant sees them and tells them to stop. He tells them that a few weeks before the same thing happened in another company and the jokesters were held for manslaughter because the victim died from fright. Are these two guilty of attempted manslaughter? Explain.

3. Arlin Roadrunner is driving along a back road late one evening when he sees a figure walking at the edge of the road ahead. As he draws closer he recognizes the figure as a former business partner who has threatened to sue Arlin because of some questionable financial transactions in the business. Arlin quickly decides to end his problems of a lawsuit by running over and killing his former partner. With this thought in mind, he picks up speed, aiming directly at the figure, intending to kill him. Just as he is about to strike the victim, the figure turns and Arlin realizes it is not his former partner. Arlin frantically swerves in an effort to avoid the person but it is too late and the victim is struck by the side of the car and seriously injured. The victim lingers close to death for several days but gradually recovers and is released from the hospital seven weeks later. Is Arlin guilty of attempted murder?

Chapter 10

Constitutional Law

Introduction

The United States Constitution is the foundation of American law and government. It is the supreme law of the land; the cornerstone of all governmental and judicial authority

As framed in the Constitutional Convention of 1787, it brought unity to a group of thirteen diverse colonies by striking a careful balance between the competing loyalties of local and national interests. Its fundamental purpose was to provide a framework for the organization of a new republic.

One of the earliest criticisms of the new Constitution was that it contained no specific guarantees of individual liberties. Ratification was secured only upon the understanding that such guarantees would be promptly added. When the first Congress convened, the House of Representatives proposed seventeen amendments in the nature of a Bill of Rights. Eventually, ten of these were finally ratified by the states in 1791.

Since then, thousands of court decisions have breathed life and strength into these founding documents. The Supreme Court, given the power to interpret the Constitution, has refined and broadened its application fare beyond the scope envisioned by its authors.

Any study of "Constitutional Law" must, of necessity, include the Constitution itself, its amendments, the Congressional enactments implementing its provisions, and the court decisions interpreting and applying it to individual cases.

Objectives

Upon completion of this chapter, you should be able to do the following:

1. Define Constitutional Law.

2. Describe how both federal and state constitutional law is created and amended.

3. Explain the judicial review function of a supreme court.

4. Describe the difference in jurisdictional scope of the federal supreme court and state supreme courts.

5. Compare the original purpose of the United States Constitution with the present application of its provisions.

6. Describe absolute and conditional rights and the significance of these terms to understanding constitutional law.

7. Briefly describe each part of the Bill of Rights, particularly the 1st, 2nd, 4th, 5th, 6th and 8th amendments.

8. Explain the meaning of "implementive provisions."

9. Explain the effects of the 14ᵗʰ amendment and the exclusionary rule.

10. Briefly describe the content of the federal civil rights acts which particularly affect law enforcement.

Lecture Notes Outline

I. Sources of law (review of chapter1)
   A. Statute law:
      1. Created by:
         a. Federal:

         b. State and local:

   B. Case law:

II. Constitutional law:
   A. Definition:

   B. Sources:
      1. Statute

	Established by:	**Amended by:**
a. Federal constitution		
b. California constitution		

10-2

2. Case Law:

C. Supreme Court functions (federal and state):
   1. Statutory interpretation:

   2. Judicial review (Marbury vs. Madison):

D. Comparison of authority of state and federal supreme courts:
   1. State:

   2. Federal:

      a. Authority to accept cases:

   3. Umbrella of Constitutional Protections:

III. Federal constitutional rights:
   A. Original intent and limitations of United States Constitution:

   B. Permanence vs. flexibility in constitution:

      1. Permanence:

      2. Flexibility:

   C. Absolute vs. conditional rights:
      1. Absolute right:

      2. Conditional right:

IV. The Bill of Rights:
   A. 1st Amendment:

      1. Religion:
         a. Establishment:

b. Free exercise:

2. Speech and press:

3. Right to assemble and petition:

B. 2nd Amendment: Right to _____.

C. 3rd Amendment:

D. 4th Amendment: Freedom from _____ and _____.

a. Authority to search granted by:

(1)

(2)

(3)

(4)

(5)

(6)

(7) _____

b. Detentions and arrests (seizures) (Review): *(Chapter 6)*
   (1) Arrests:

   (2) Detentions:

E. 5th Amendment:
   1. Grand jury prosecution:

   2. Double jeopardy:

   3. Self-incrimination:

a. Does not apply to:

  (1)

  (2)

b. Miranda vs. Arizona (outgrowth of 5th and 6th amendments):
   (1) Applies to:

   (2) Warning required:

     (a)

     (b)

     (c)

     (d)

4. Due process:

  a. Substantive due process:

  b. Procedural due process:

5. Eminent domain:

F. 6th Amendment:
   1. Trial procedures:
      a. Speedy trial:

      b. Jury trial:
         (1) When required:

         (2) Number of jurors:

         (3) Verdict requirement:

   2. Right to counsel:

   3. Right to confront accusers and call witnesses:

G. 7th Amendment:

H. 8th Amendment:
   1. Bail:

2. Punishment:

    a. Capital punishment:

I. 9th Amendment:

J. 10th Amendment:

V. Implementive provisions:
    A. General:

    B. Civil rights acts and other federal legislation:
      1. Title 18, United States Code, section 241 (Conspiracy to violate Constitutional Rights of anyone):

        a. Elements:

          (1) _____ persons who _____ to

          (2) injure, threaten, oppress or intimidate any _____.

          (3) in the free exercise of rights or privileges granted by U.S. Constitution or U.S. law,

        b. Penalty:

2. Title 18, United States Code, section 242 (Misuse of authority):

   a. Elements:

      (1) Willfully depriving another person of rights protected by Constitution or other U.S. law,

      (2) under _____ of _____, or

      (3) subjects them to different _____

      _____

      _____.

   b. Penalty:

3. Comparison between 18 USC 241 and 18 USC 242:

   a.

   b.

4. Enforcement (18 USC 245):

5. Federal Civil Rights Civil Liability Act (42 USC 1983):

C. 14th Amendment (1868):

   1. Places limits on _____ government.

      a.

      b.

      c.

D. Exclusionary rule:
   1. Definition:

   2. History:

      1914 – Weeks vs. U.S.:

      1949 – Wolfe vs. Colorado:

      1955 – People vs. Cahan (California):

      1961 – Mapp vs. Ohio:

   3. Intent and Effect of exclusionary rule:

Reading Assignment

None.

Definitions

Define and/or explain the following:
A. constitutional law:

B. implementive provisions:

C. statutory interpretation:

D. due process:

E. judicial review:

F. absolute and conditional rights:

G. exclusionary rule:

Chapter Problems

True – False:

1. The United States Constitution can be amended by a 2/3 vote of the voters in a National Election.

2. The California State Constitution contains some of the same provisions as the United States Constitution.

3. The California State Constitution may be amended by a 2/3 vote of the legislature followed by a majority vote of the voters of the state.

4. All provisions of the Bill of Rights apply to California State Agencies.

5. The rights established by the Bill of Rights are not absolute; they have many limitations and conditions imposed by Supreme Court decisions.

6. The Constitution guarantees the right to a jury trial in all criminal cases.

7. "Judicial Review" means the right of the Supreme Court to determine the constitutional validity of laws passed by the Legislatures or Congress.

8. A defendant in a California case is convicted of burglary for breaking into a pay phone booth. He is argues that a phone booth is not a building and therefore does not fall under the law of burglary. The California Supreme Court rules that a phone booth is a "Building" and upholds the conviction. The defendant may have the United States Supreme Court review the California Court's definition of a "Building."

9. The original intent of the authors of the United States Constitution was to protect United States citizens from excesses of state and local police agencies.

10. The first amendment right of freedom of the press, permits a newspaper to print any statement, regardless of its accuracy, without fear of a lawsuit.

11. A private citizen does have a constitutional right to own a handgun.

12. The 4th Amendment prohibits unreasonable searches.

13. The "Miranda Decision" is an outgrowth of the 5th and 6th Amendments.

14. The 5th Amendment protects against self-incrimination.

15. The right to "Life, Liberty and the pursuit of Happiness" is part of the first ten Amendments to the United States Constitution.

16. The United States Constitution has been applied to the states on a case-by-case and section-by-section basis, rather than all at the same time.

17. "Implementive provisions" are the laws and case decisions which give effect to the Constitution.

18. The 14th Amendment has served to apply the Bill of Rights to the states.

19. The 14th Amendment is one of the few parts of the Constitution which was specifically intended to apply only to the actions of the federal government.

20. The Exclusionary Rule is a rule of evidence which prohibits the use in court of evidence which was obtained in violation of the protection granted by any part of the Constitution.

Bill of Rights and 14th Amendment

I

Congress shall make no law respecting an establishment of religion, or prohibiting the free exercise thereof; or abridging the freedom of speech, or of the press, or the right of the people peaceably to assemble, and to petition the Government for a redress of grievances.

II

A well–regulated militia, being necessary to the security of a free State, the right of the people to keep and bear arms, shall not be infringed.

III

No soldier shall, in time of peace be quartered in any house, without the consent of the owner, nor in time of war, but in a manner to be prescribed by law.

IV

The right of the people to be secure in their persons, houses, papers, and effects, against unreasonable searches and seizures, shall not be violated, and no Warrants shall issue, but upon probable cause, supported by oath or affirmation, and particularly describing the place to be searched, and the persons or things to be seized.

V

No person shall be held to answer for a capital, or otherwise infamous crime, unless on a presentment or indictment of a Grand Jury, except in cases arising in the land or naval forces, or in the Militia, when in actual service in time of War or public danger; nor shall any person be subject for the same offense to be twice put in jeopardy of life or limb; nor shall be compelled in any criminal case to be a witness against himself, nor be deprived of life, liberty, or property, without due process of law; nor shall private property be taken for public use without just compensation.

VI

In all criminal prosecutions, the accused shall enjoy the right to a speedy and public trial, by an impartial jury of the State and district wherein the crime shall have been committed, which district shall have been previously ascertained by law, and to be informed of the nature and cause of the accusation; to be confronted with the witnesses against him; to have compulsory process for obtaining witnesses in his favor, and to have the assistance of counsel for his defense.

VII

In suits at common law, where the value in controversy shall exceed twenty dollars, the right of trial by jury shall be preserved, and no fact tried by a jury shall be otherwise re–examined in any court of the United States, than according to the rules of the common law.

VIII

Excessive bail shall not be required nor excessive fines imposed, nor cruel and unusual punishments inflicted.

IX

The enumeration in the Constitution, of certain rights, shall not be construed to deny or disparage others retained by the people.

X

The powers not delegated to the United States by the Constitution, nor prohibited by it to the States, are reserved to the States respectively, or to the people.

XIV

Section 1.
All persons born or naturalized in the United States, and subject to the jurisdiction thereof, are citizens of the United States and of the State wherein they reside. No State shall make or enforce any law which shall abridge the privileges or immunities of citizens of the United States; nor shall any State deprive any person of life, liberty, or property, without due process of law; nor deny to any person within its jurisdiction the equal protection of the laws.

Section 2.
Representatives shall be apportioned among the several States according to their respective numbers, counting the whole number of persons in each State, excluding Indians not taxed. But when the right to vote at any election for the choice of electors for President and Vice-President of the United States, Representatives in Congress, the Executive and Judicial officers of a State, or the members of the Legislature thereof, is denied to any of the male inhabitants of such State, being twenty-one years of age,* and citizens of the United States, or in any way abridged, except for participation in rebellion, or other crime, the basis of representation therein shall be reduced in the proportion which the number of such male citizens shall bear to the whole number of male citizens twenty-one years of age in such State.

Section 3.
No person shall be a Senator or Representative in Congress, or elector of President and Vice-President, or hold any office, civil or military, under the United States, or under any State, who, having previously taken an oath, as a member of Congress, or as an officer of the United States, or as a member of any State legislature, or as an executive or judicial officer of any State, to support the Constitution of the United States, shall have engaged in insurrection or rebellion against the same, or given aid or comfort to the enemies thereof. But Congress may by a vote of two-thirds of each House, remove such disability.

Section 4.
The validity of the public debt of the United States, authorized by law, including debts incurred for payment of pensions and bounties for services in suppressing insurrection or rebellion, shall not be questioned. But neither the United States nor any State shall assume or pay any debt or obligation incurred in aid of insurrection or rebellion against the United States, or any claim for the loss or emancipation of any slave; but all such debts, obligations and claims shall be held illegal and void.

Section 5.
The Congress shall have the power to enforce, by appropriate legislation, the provisions of this article.

Part II

California Substantive Criminal Law

The purpose of the Substantive Criminal Law course is to provide you with a working knowledge of the most serious and most frequently encountered California crimes. It examines both the statutory elements of these crimes as well as the case law interpretations applied by the California appellate courts. In addition, it provides guidance for the reasonable and realistic enforcement of these laws. This course is designed as the second of two one-semester classes introducing criminal law. The prerequisite first semester course is Concepts of Criminal Law, which provides an understanding of the fundamental principles of criminal law. This course extends that knowledge and also provides an opportunity to apply it to specific crimes.

A. Categories of Crimes described in Substantive Criminal Law:

1. Crimes Against Persons
   (assault, battery, ADW, sex crimes, kidnapping, murder, etc.)

2. Crimes Against Property
   (burglary, theft, robbery, forgery, etc.)

3. Crimes Against Government Institutions
   (perjury, bribery, etc.)

4. Crimes Against Public Peace and Order
   (riot, disturbing the peace, unlawful assembly, etc.)

5. Crimes Against Public Morals and Safety
   (narcotics, prostitution, gambling, etc.)

Important note regarding penalties:

With a few exceptions, penalties are not emphasized in this course. Although an officer should know the classification (felony or misdemeanor) of crimes in order to make a lawful arrest, officers are not involved in sentencing, and do not need to be aware of exact penalties. Also, penalties are so complex and change so frequently, it is impossible to remain current.

P.O.S.T. LEARNING DOMAINS AND TRAINING SPECIFICATIONS:

The content of this course outline satisfies all of the requirements of the following P.O.S.T. Learning Domains of the Regular Basic Course:

#6 – Property Crimes – 10 hours

#7 – Crimes Against Persons – 10 hours

#8 – General Criminal Statutes – 4 hours

#9 – Crimes Against Children – 6 hours

#10 – Sex Crimes – 6 hours

#39 – Crimes Against the Justice System – 4 hours

#40 – Weapons Violations – 4 hours

Chapter 11

Homicide

Introduction

Probably the most malicious act of man is that of taking the life of another human being. Of all the adversity that man inflicts on man, this is the ultimate. Property damage can be repaired; physical injuries can heal; stolen goods can be returned or replaced; a burned building can be rebuilt; but the life that is ended can never be restored.

Despite its seriousness, this crime has existed throughout all of recorded history, and archeological discoveries indicate that deliberate homicides occurred even before man was capable of leaving a written record of his deed.

Murder has been a favorite subject of literature from the Biblical account of Cain and Abel, through Sherlock Holmes and Perry Mason, to the most recent episode of television's current cloak and dagger thriller.

This preoccupation with bloodshed by almost every segment of society may account for the more than thirty thousand deliberate killings which take place in the United States every year. In the Los Angeles area alone, there is an average of over six murders every twenty-four hours.

Included in this chapter is a brief section on abortion.

Objectives

Upon completing this chapter, you should be able to briefly describe the current laws on abortion and give a detailed explanation of the law of homicide, including:

A. Types of homicides

B. The elements of murder, manslaughter and related crimes

C. Proof of death

D. Legal causation in homicides

E. Types of malice

F. Degrees of murder

G. Penalties for murder and manslaughter

Lecture Notes Outline

I. Homicide defined:

    A. Lawful homicides (_____ or _____)

        1. Excusable:

        2. Justifiable:

    B. Unlawful homicide: (_____ or_____)

        1. Common elements of both murder and manslaughter:

            a. A human being, _____ _____ ;

            b. is now _____ ; (_____)

            c. with the death caused by the _____ .

        2. Investigative Responsibilities:

II. General rules of unlawful homicides:
    A. Proof of death:
        1. Circumstantial evidence:

2. Recovery of dead body:

3. Defendant's confession:

B. Cause of death:
  1. Act and intent rules:
     a. Responsibility for direct and foreseeable results (proximate cause):

     b. Dual causes:

  2. Preexisting conditions:

C. Time limit in homicides:
  1. Statutory limit (194 PC):

  2. How calculated:

D. Definition of "human":

   1. Unborn infant:

      a. For manslaughter:

         (1)

         (2)

         (3)

      b. For murder:

   2. Dead body:

      a. Vital functions:

         (1)

         (2)

         (3)

      b. Legal Death (7180 H & S Code):

III.   Murder (187 PC):

A. Definition: The _____ killing of a human being or _____

_____ , with _____ _____ .

B. Malice:

1. Types of malice:

a.

b.

2. Circumstances which satisfy the malice element of the corpus delicti of murder:

a.   Intent to _____ .

b. Intent to cause _____ _____ .

c. Intent to do something which is _____ _____ to cause

_____ or _____ _____ .

d. Intent to commit a _____ _____ which results in death to another.
      (Felony Murder Rule)

e. Intent to forcibly _____ _____ .

C. Definition of aforethought:

IV. Degrees of murder:

A. First degree murder:

1. Type of intent:

W _____ , D _____ and

P _____ intent to _____ .

a. Premeditation:

2. Method used:

a. P _____ ;

b. T _____ ;

c. L _____ in W _____ ;

d. B _____ ;

e. A _____ P _____ ammunition;

3. F _____ M _____ R _____ :

    B. _____

    A. _____

    R. _____

    R. _____

    M. _____

288. _____

    K. _____

    V. _____ H. _____

    D. _____ Shooting

    K. _____

B. Second Degree Murder:

V. Penalties for Murder (190 PC et al):
  A. First Degree Murder:
    1. Without Death Sentence Special Circumstances:

      a. Parole:

    2. Murder of a Public Transport Operator (190.23 PC):

    3. Death Sentence and Life Without Parole:
      a. Limitations:
        (1) In Felony murder rule cases:

        (2) Application to co-principals:

(3) Age:

b. Special Circumstances for Death Sentence (190.2 PC):

    (1) Killing a peace officer, firefighter, judge, D.A., prison guard and other designated government officials.

    (2) Hired killer (paid to kill another).

    (3) Multiple murders or prior murder conviction.

    (4) Murder of a court witness.

    (5) Killing while resisting arrest or escaping from custody.

    (6) Death caused by train wreck, explosives, poison, torture or armor piercing ammunition.

    (7) Death caused during a:

        (a) Burglary

        (b) Arson

        (c) Rape or other sex crime

        (d) Robbery

        (e) Kidnapping

        (f) Child molesting

    (8) Murder related to civil rights:

        (a) Based on race, religion, color, nationality, gender or sexual orientation.

c. Death Penalty procedures:
    (1) Charges:

    (2) Guilt phase of trial:

        (a)

        (b)

(3) Penalty phase of trial:

    (a) Jury Decision:
       (i) Against death sentence:

       (ii) For death sentence:

    (b) Modification by Judge:

    (c) Automatic Review:

B. Second degree murder:

VI. Manslaughter (192 PC):
  A. Defined:

  B. Types:

    1.

    2.

    3.

  C. Voluntary manslaughter:
    1. Definition and concepts:

2. Heat of Passion Theory:
   a. Requirements:

   (1)

   (2)

   (3)

3. Diminished Capacity Theory:

D. Involuntary Manslaughter:
   1. Types:

      a.

      b.

E. Penalty for manslaughter (193 PC):

   1. Voluntary:

   2. Involuntary:

F. Motor vehicle manslaughter:
   1. Requirements:

      a.

      b.

11-10

c.

2. Penalty variations:

a. Gross negligence:

(1) Penalty:
   (a) while under the influence:

   (b) not under the influence:

b. ordinary negligence:

(1) Penalty:
   (a) while under the influence:

   (b) not under the influence:

G. Civil Liability:

VII. Abortion (274 PC):
   A. Background:

   B. California Therapeutic Abortion Act (25950 H and S):

VIII. Aiding a suicide (401 PC):

Reading Assignment

1. California Penal Code Sections: 187 – 199, 274, 275, 276, 401 and 1108.
2. Health and Safety Code: 25950.

Definitions

Define or explain the following:

A. homicide:

B. matricide:

C. patricide:

D. fratricide:

E. excusable homicide:

F. justifiable homicide:

G. murder:

H. manslaughter:

I. expressed malice:

J. implied malice:

K. malice aforethought:

L. torture:

M. abortion:

Supplemental Reading

Homicide Study Guide

Investigation of a homicide can be extremely complicated. The fine distinctions between justifiable and excusable homicide, voluntary and involuntary manslaughter, and first and second-degree murder can confuse the most experienced investigator.

The following checklist provides a step-by-step guide through the legal complexities involved in homicide problems. Each of these questions must be considered in evaluating a homicide case.

☐ 1. Is the defendant the legal cause of the victim's death?

    ☐ a. Is there any legal problem related to the defendant's failure to fulfill some duty to the victim? (If the death was caused by the defendant's failure to take some action, did the defendant have a duty which required him or her to act?)

    ☐ b. Did the victim have any preexisti9ng health condition? (This does not provide a defense.)

    ☐ c. Was the defendant's conduct the direct and proximate cause of the victim's death? (Is there a close enough relationship between the defendant's actions and the victim's death? Was the result foreseeable?)

    ☐ d. Did the victim die within the three-year and a day time limit?

    ☐ e. Was the victim alive at the time of the defendant's act? (pre-birth or post-death problems)

☐ 2. Is the death an act of murder? (Is there expressed or implied malice?)

    ☐ a. Was there a deliberate, premeditated intent to kill?

    ☐ b. Was there an intent to cause great bodily injury?

    ☐ c. Did the defendant intend to commit an act highly likely to cause death or great bodily injury?

    ☐ d. Does the felony murder rule apply?

    ☐ e. Was the defendant forcefully resisting arrest?

    Need any one condition. (applies to a–e)

☐ 3. If the act appears to be murder, are there any mitigating circumstances to reduce the act to voluntary manslaughter?

    ☐ a. Heat of Passion Theory:

        ☐ (1) Uncontrollable passion.

        ☐ (2) Adequate provocation.

        ☐ (3) No period of cooling.

        Need all three conditions.

    ☐ b. Diminished Capacity Theory.

☐ 4. If there are no mitigating circumstances to reduce the crime to voluntary manslaughter, does it meet the requirements of Involuntary Manslaughter?

    ☐ a. Misdemeanor Manslaughter Rule.

    ☐ b. Criminal Negligence.

☐ 5. If the killing satisfies the requirements to be murder, and there are no circumstances which would reduce it to manslaughter, what degree of murder has occurred?

    ☐ a. First degree?

        ☐ (1) Willful, deliberate, premeditated intent to kill?

        ☐ (2) By use of a bomb, poison, torture, lying in wait or armor piercing ammo?

        ☐ (3) During the commission of a BARRM-288, K, Vehicle High Jacking or Drive-by Shooting.

        } Need any one circumstance.

    ☐ b. If first degree murder, do the death sentence special circumstances exist?

    ☐ c. Second degree?

        ☐ (1) All other murders.

☐ 6. Is it motor vehicle manslaughter?

    ☐ a. Through commission of a misdemeanor or by negligence.

        ☐ (1) With gross negligence.

        ☐ (2) Without gross negligence.

☐ 7. Is there any excuse, justification or defense? If not, the defendant is guilty of the highest crime which fits the facts of the case.

Chapter Problems

1. Butch sees his lifelong enemy, Fred, walking along the road. In a fraction of a second, Butch decides to run him over with his car, hoping that the death of Fred will appear to be an accident. Fred is walking almost in the center of the road as Butch bears down on him. Fred hears Butch's car just in time to leap out of the way. He lands in the ditch beside the road however, and injures his leg. Butch comes back and helps Fred, who believes it was just an accident and unavoidable as the night was very dark. Fred goes to a hospital for treatment but one month later the leg develops an infection from the injury and Fred dies.

   Is Butch guilty of any type of homicide? Explain your answer fully.

2. Philomena Pillhead has been a heavy drug user for the past three years. Recently, her excesses have reached the point of causing occasional severe emotional outbursts. During these outbursts she has injured herself and others in wild fights. Later, she has always shown regret and sorrow for hurting others. Her part time boyfriend and pill supplier is Harry the Hype. Philomena has learned that Harry is running around with other women and has threatened severe reprisal if she catches him at it. Last Friday evening, Harry was found dead in his apartment, shot through the chest. Philomena is found wandering the street about eight blocks away in a semi-hysterical condition. She is high on drugs at the time. The gun which fired the fatal shot is found in her purse. She admits shooting Harry but continues to say "I didn't mean it" throughout the questioning.

   Based on these facts, Philomena might be guilty of some type of criminal homicide or she might be innocent, depending on what additional facts are uncovered in the investigation. Use your imagination to formulate four different sets of additional facts, consistent with the above, which would show that Philomena is:

   1. Guilty of first-degree murder.
   2. Guilty of second-degree murder.
   3. Guilty of voluntary manslaughter.
   4. Not guilty of Harry's death, because she has a complete defense.

3. Pete gets into an argument with Paul over the affections of Mary and Pete shoots Paul, intending to kill him. The shooting takes place on January 6, 1995, and Paul goes to the hospital where he remains in serious condition for a long period of time. Mary jilts them both and marries Dick who is not as good looking but has lots of money from his job as a school teacher. On January 7, 1998, Paul is still in the hospital from the original wound and Pete goes to visit him. Paul kids Pete about the fact that he was jilted and Pete, sensitive and irritated about it, tells him to stop. Paul continues and Pete, after carefully and calmly looking for a suitable weapon, hits Paul over the head with a bedpan, intending to knock Paul unconscious and thus stop the talk. Paul, because of his weakened condition from being in a hospital for over three years, dies from the blow.
   a. As a D.A. what charges will you file against Pete?

   b. Explain why:

   c. As Pete's attorney, how will you defend him?

4. George gets into an argument with Sam's wife and slugs her in the face. Sam, when he hears about it flies into a rage and swears to kill George. He is finally calmed down by his friends. The following week, Sam intends to get even with George by doing the same thing to George's wife Gertrude. He goes to George's house, intending to hit Gertrude in the face. Gertrude sees Sam coming and tries to hide. This enrages Sam who pulls out a knife and starts to chase Gertrude with the intention of slashing her face. Gertrude runs out the back door and almost gets away but slips on the pavement, falls down and strikes her head and is killed.
   a. Is Sam guilty of any type of homicide? Explain.

   b. As Sam's attorney, what are the best defense arguments?

5. Alvin has been secretly dating Wilbur's girlfriend, Zelda. When Wilbur learns about this, he vows to get even with both of them. That night, he hides in some bushes near Zelda's house. He sees two people sitting closely together on the couch, in Zelda's living room. When they lean together to embrace, Wilbur suddenly grabs a brick and throws it through the living room window. The brick hits and kills Carmichael who was sitting on the couch with Zelda's sister, Zephyr. Alvin and Zelda were not in the house at the time.
   1. If you were the D.A., what is the highest possible charge you can file against Wilbur and on what theory?

   2. If you were Wilbur's attorney, what is your best defense argument and what legal result do you hope to achieve with it?

   3. As the D.A., how would you counter the defense argument presented above?

Chapter 12

Battery and Assaults

Introduction

The phrase "assault and battery" has found such wide use that most laymen assume that it refers to one single criminal act. Actually, the crime of "assault" is separate and distinct from the crime of "battery," although frequently both will be committed at the same time. Also, there are several different types of assaults, and at least two forms of battery.

Although certainly not as serious as the homicides which you have just studied, assaults and related crimes are far more numerous and cover a much wider range of undesirable behavior. An assault or battery can consist of anything from a minor jostling to a violently inflicted injury falling just short of killing the victim.

Objectives

Upon completing this chapter, you should be able to describe in detail all of the laws related to the crimes of:

1. Battery.

2. Simple assault.

3. Assault with a deadly weapon.

4. Other felonious assaults.

5. Other crimes related to assaults.

Lecture Notes Outline

I. Battery (242 PC):

A. Definitions and elements:

1.

2.

3.

4.

B. Analysis:

    1. Force: *(2nd element)*

      a. Definition:

      b. Examples:

    2. Person of another: *(3rd element)*

    3. Willful and unlawful: *(1st element)*

    4. Without consent: *(4th element)*

      a. Implied consent:

      b. Specific consent:

      c. Invalid consent:

d. Authority in lieu of consent:

    (1)

    (2)

    (3)

C. Punishment (243 PC):
  1. General:

  2. If serious injury results:

  3. Against a peace officer, lifeguard, EMT or firefighter:

D. Sexual battery (243.4 PC): (Complete description in Chapter 14)

II. Simple assault (240 PC):
  A. Definition:

  B. Elements:

    1.

    2.

    3.

  C. Analysis of elements:
    1. Intent to batter:

    2. Act toward a battery:

3. Actual present ability:

D. Penalty (241 PC):

1. General:

2. Against a peace officer, lifeguard, EMT or firefighter (241 (b), 243 (b) PC):

3. Against a cab or bus driver or on school property (241.2, 241.3 PC):

4. Other:

III. Assault with a deadly weapon (ADW) (245 PC):
A. General comparison of felonious assaults with simple assault and battery:

B. Types of ADW:
1.

2.

C. Analysis of ADW:
1. Use of a deadly weapon:
a. Type of weapon:

b. Intent:

2. Force likely to produce great bodily injury:
   a. General:

   (1) Professional fighter:

D. ADW Penalty:
   1. General (245(a)(i) PC):

   2. Against a peace officer or firefighter (245b PC);

      a. general:

      b. with a firearm:

   3. Against a bus or cab driver (245.2 PC):

   4. Against a custodial officer (245.3 PC):

IV. Assault with intent to commit a felony (220 PC):
    A. General:

B. Elements:

   1.

   2.

C. Felonies included:

D. Penalty: *2, 4 or 6 years.*

V. Other types of assaults:
  A. Assault with a caustic chemical or acid (244 PC):
    1. Elements:

      a.

      b.

      c.

      d.

    2. Penalty:

  B. ADW or battery by a state prison inmate (4500 to 4501 PC):
    1. General:

    2. Punishment:

      a. Normal ADW penalty, outside prison:

      b. By a prison inmate serving less than life:

      c. Inmate serving life sentence:

    3. Battery by a state prison inmate:

VI. Related crimes:
   A. Involving poisons:
     1. Administering a narcotic or intoxicant for the purpose of committing a felony (222 PC):

     2. Poisoning food, drink, medicine or water (347 PC):

   B. Involving vehicles:
     1. Train wrecking (218 and 219 PC):

     2. Wrecking a public carrier (219.1 PC):

     3. Throwing an object at a public carrier (219.2 PC):

     4. Throwing an object at a vehicle (23110 VC):

   C. Involving weapons:
     1. Possession of a weapon with the intent to assault (17500 PC):

     2. Possession of a switchblade knife (21510 PC):

3. Electric Shock Weapons (244.5 PC):

4. Discharging a firearm at an occupied or inhabited building or vehicle (246 PC):

5. Firing at an unoccupied building, aircraft or vehicle (247 PC):

6. Discharging a firearm with gross negligence (246.3 PC):

7. Exhibiting a firearm or other weapon (417 – 417.8 PC):

VII. Stalking (Threatening Violence) (646.9 PC):
   A. Elements:
      1. Willfully, maliciously and _____,

      2. _____ or _____ any person,

      3. which causes the victim _____.
         _____.

   B. Restraining order:

   C. Penalty:

VIII. Child, Spouse and Elder Abuse:
    A. Child Endangering (Child Neglect) (273a PC):
       1. Elements:

          a. _____ any child to suffer unjustifiable physical pain

          or _____ suffering ... OR ...

          b. Having _____ or _____ of a child,

            (1) _____ such injury, or

            (2)

       2. Penalty:

    B. Child Abuse (273d PC):
       1. Elements:
          a. Willfully inflicting _____ punishment, resulting in

          _____ injury to a child.

         (1) Type of injury:

         (2) Relationship to child:

       2. Valid parental discipline:

          a. School officials:

       3. Penalty:

    C. Spousal Abuse (273.5 PC):
       1. Inflicting _____ injury

2. To: (Relationships)

   a.

   b.

   c.

3. Penalty:

D. Battery of a former spouse, fiancé or person in a dating relationship (243(e) PC):
   1. Comparison with battery (242 PC):
      a. Violation of trust:

      b. Penalty:

E. Special spousal abuse prevention laws (273.5 – 273.87 PC & 13700 – 13710 PC):
   1. Funding:

   2. Training:

   3. Enforcement policies:

   4. Restraining Orders:

   5. Effects of special abuse prevention laws:

F. Abuse of Elderly and Dependent adults (368 PC & 15630 WIC):
   1. Definitions:
      a. Dependent adult:

      b. Elder:

      c. Abuse:

      d. Neglect:

2. Elements:

    a. Willfully _____ or _____

    b. any _____ or _____ _____

    c. to suffer _____

    _____.

    d. or _____

    e. Or _____

3. Penalty:

Reading Assignment

1. California Penal Code Sections: 218 – 219.3, 220 – 222, 240 – 247, 273.5 – 273.87, 273a, 273d, 273.6 – 273.87, 347, 4500, 4501, 4501.5, 347, 386, 417 – 417.8, 273, 273.5, 594, 646.9, 1000.6 – 1000.10, , 13700 – 13731,17500, 21510.

Definitions

Define or explain the following:

A. Battery:

B. Implied consent:

C. Assault:

D. Assault with a deadly weapon:

E. Traumatic injury:

Chapter Problems

True or false – circle the best answer here and on the answer sheet.

1. T   F   Kissing someone who objected to it would be a battery.

2. T   F   Deliberately leaving a mousetrap with the intent that someone would catch his fingers in it would not be battery even if the victim was injured because there would be no direct touching of the victim by the defendant.

3. T   F   Deliberately throwing sand at someone on the beach is not a battery because this is the type of activity that a lot of people engage in and anyone who objects should leave rather than just complain.

4. T   F   A battery is always a misdemeanor.

5. T   F   Sam throws a small rock at Charlie, intending to hit him because of a recent fight between the two. The rock misses and Charlie is never aware of the danger because his back was turned at the time. Sam is still guilty of at least a simple assault.

6. T   F   Paul jumps from behind a tree and shouts at Wilmer, scaring him severely. Paul is guilty of an assault.

7. T   F   A professional boxer's hands are always considered to be deadly weapons.

8. T   F   It is necessary that an actual weapon be used in order for a person to be guilty of assault with a deadly weapon (245 PC).

9. T   F   In the crime of exhibiting a firearm in a threatening manner (217 PC) it is not necessary that the gun be loaded.

10. T   F   In a violation of section 273.5 PC (spouse beating) it is necessary to prove that the parties are legally married.

Chapter 13

Crimes of Restraint

Introduction

There are a number of crimes in which restraint of the victim is a common element. These crimes range from minor misdemeanors to one capital offense. In addition to recognizing these crimes for investigative and enforcement purposes, peace officers should be aware that, through lack of knowledge, they could violate one of these statutes themselves.

Objectives

Upon completing this chapter you should be able to list and explain in detail all of the elements of the various crimes involving restraint of the victim, including:

False imprisonment
Kidnapping
False arrest
Child stealing

Lecture Notes Outline

I. False imprisonment (236 PC):
   A. Definition:

   An act of force, or _____ of force, which deprives another of their _____

   without _____ _____ .

   B. Analysis of corpus delicti:
      1. Act or threat of force:

2. Depriving another of liberty:
   a. Freedom of choice:

   b. Reasonable means of escape:

3. Without lawful authority:

   a. Burden of Proof:

C. Penalty:
  1. Normal:

  2. Accomplished by the use of force, violence, threat or deceit:

II. Kidnapping (207 PC):
  A. Definition:

  B. Types of kidnapping: *(4 types)*
   1. Forcibly imprisoning and moving the victim:

   2. Forcibly imprisoning someone with the intent to take him or her out of the state:

3. Persuading a person to leave the state through false promises:

4. Bringing a kidnap victim into the state:

C. Penalty:

III. Kidnapping for robbery, ransom or extortion (209 PC):
A. Elements:

B. Penalty:
1. Without harm to victim:

2. With physical harm to the victim:

a. Definition of "physical harm":

3. With death of the victim (Little Lindberg Law) (187 PC):

C. Federal Kidnapping Law (18 USC 1201):

IV. Posing as a kidnapper (210 PC):
A. Definition:

B. Penalty:

V. False arrest:

    A. Criminal (146 PC):

        1. Penalty:

    B. Civil:

VI. Child Stealing (278 PC):
    A. Corpus delicti:

        1.

        2.

        3.

        4.

    B. Intent:

    C. Distinguished from kidnapping:

    D. Penalty:
        1. Normal (278 PC):

        2. If committed by a parent or guardian contrary to a child custody court order (278.5 PC):

Reading Assignment

1. California Penal Code Sections: 236, 237, 207 – 210, 146, 278, 279, 280 PC.

Definitions

Explain or define the following:

A. False Imprisonment:

B. Kidnapping:

C. Little Lindberg Law:

D. False Arrest:
  1. Criminal:

  2. Civil:

E. Child Stealing:

Chapter Problems

1. In order for a defendant to receive a death penalty under the "Little Lindberg Law," what circumstances must exist? (Write your answer in outline form.)

2. What is the difference between the crime of false arrest and the civil tort of false arrest?

3. What is the penalty for simple kidnapping under section 207 PC?

4. What is included in the definition of "bodily harm" as required under section 209 PC?

5. Who is considered to be the injured party or victim in a child stealing case (278 PC)?

Chapter 14

Sex Offenses

Introduction

The sexual offenses are among the oldest of crimes. They have existed in every period of recorded history and in every country of the world. Whether a particular sexual act is viewed as a crime or not will vary considerably from one country to another however, depending on the social customs in each country.

A sex crime is unique. It involves deep human emotions and the perpetrator will frequently border on the psychopathic. Most crimes are motivated by either a desire for material wealth (theft, robbery, burglary) or a hatred for the victim (assault, battery, murder). Sex crimes have a much more complex motivation. A sex crime results from an overpowering desire to satisfy the natural human sex drive in an unnatural manner or a compulsion to humiliate and degrade the victim.

A detective investigating a sex crime must maintain an objective, professional demeanor and must learn and use acceptable professional vocabulary in interviewing victims and witnesses. The investigator must be patient and sympathetic in dealing with victims of these crimes.

Women studying this material should be mindful that it is a common practice to assign policewomen to the investigation of crimes against women and children, thus they will frequently be dealing with sex offenses.

Objectives

Upon completing this chapter you should be able to provide a detailed explanation of the crimes of rape, child molesting, sex perversion, incest and other related sex offenses.

Lecture Notes Outline

I. Introduction
   A. Subject:

II. Importance of subject:
   A. Frequency and seriousness of offenses:

B. Nature of sex crimes:
    1. Unique objectives of sex crime laws:

        a. Most criminal laws protect individuals from:

        b. Sex crimes:
           (1) Protect an individual's:

    2. Unique motivations of sex criminals:
        a. Motivation for most crimes:

           (1)

           (2)

        b. Sex crimes involve complex motivations:

           (1)

           (2)

           (3)

           (4)

C. Complications of sex crime laws:
    1. Nature of damage:

    2. Emotional nature of sex crimes:

D. Difficulty in creating sex crime laws (Legislature):

E. Difficulty in interpreting laws and punishing offenders (Courts):

F. Difficulty in enforcement (police and prosecutor):
   1. Danger of false accusations:

   2. Enforcement policy: letter of the law or desires of the community and parties involved?

   3. Investigation of sex crimes:
      a. Demeanor:

      b. Vocabulary:

      c. Objectivity:

      d. Sensitivity:

Criminal Sections:

I. Rape (261 PC):
   A. Definition:

   B. General rules:
      1. Male perpetrator:

      2. Sexual penetration (263 PC):

      3. Chastity of the victim:

         a. Rape evidence law:

      4. Corroboration:

      5. Statute of limitations:

   C. Forms of rape (261 PC):
      1. Forcible rape (261(2) PC):

a. Resistance by the victim:

2. Rape by threat (261(6) PC):

    a. Resistance by the victim:

3. Use of alcohol or drugs (261(3) PC):

4. Victim of unsound mind (261 (1) PC):

5. Victim unconscious of nature of act (261(4) PC):

6. Victim believes assailant is her husband (261 (5) PC):

7. Threat of arrest or other legal action (261 (7) PC):

D. Related crime:
   1. Unlawful intercourse with a minor (formerly statutory rape) (261.5 PC):
      a. Elements:

         (1)

         (2)

         (3)

      b. Defenses:

      c. Practical aspects of enforcement:

E. Penalties (264 PC):
   1. Rape:
      a. Normal:

      b. Group rape:

   2. Unlawful intercourse:

F. Spousal Rape (262 PC):

    1. Reporting requirement:

    2. Penalty:

II. Sexual Battery (2453.4 PC):
    A. Elements:

       1.

       2.

       3.

       4.

    B. Penalty:

III. Sexual assault with an object (289 PC):
    A. Elements:

       1.

       2.

       3.

       4.

       5.

    B. Penalty:

IV. Sexual Assault on an Animal (286.5 PC):

    A. Description:

    B. Penalty:

V. Incest (285 PC):
    A. Definition:

    B. Background and objectives:

    C. Prohibited relationships (4400 Civil Code):

        1.

        2.

        3.

    D. Does not prohibit marriage or sexual relations between:

    E. Penalty:

    F. Additional crimes:
        1. Against victim:

        2. Performing an incestuous marriage (359 PC):

VI. Sodomy (286 PC):
   A. Original Definition:

   B. Present Definition:

   C. Legal Background:

   D. Penalties:
      1. Victim under _____.

      2. Victim under _____ and defendant over _____ .

      3. Victim under _____ and defendant more than _____ years older.

      4. Victim physically forced:

      5. _____ or more defendants, using _____ against the victim.

VII. Unlawful Oral Copulation (288a PC):
   A. Definition:

   B. Legal history:

   C. Condition under which act is a crime:

      1.

      2.

      3.

D. Penalty:
    1. Variables:
        a.

        b.

        c.

    2. Range of penalties:

VIII. Child molesting (288 and 647.6 PC):
    A. Elements:
        1. _____ or lascivious acts upon the _____

        2. of a child under the age of _____

          a. Sex of the parties:

        3. with the intent of arousing or satisfying the _____ _____ of

        _____ _____ .

          a. Satisfaction of intent:

        4. Penalty:

    B. Child molesting (misdemeanor – 647.6 PC):
        1. Elements:
          a. Act:

          b. Age of child:

          c. Intent:

        2. Penalty:
          a. Normal:

          b. With prior convictions:

C. Continuous Sexual Abuse of A Child (288.5 PC):
  1. Elements:
    a. Any person who has:

    b. With a minor under _____ …

    c. And who engages in _____ acts of: _____.

    d. Over a period of at least _____ months …

  2. Penalty:

IX. Bigamy (281 PC):
A. Definition:

B. Exceptions:

C. Penalty for bigamy:

D. Single person marrying another who is already married (284 PC):

  1. Description:

  2. Penalty:

X. Fornication and adultery:

XI. Lewd Conduct:
    A. Indecent exposure (314 PC):
       1. Elements:

          a.

          b.

          c.

       2. Penalty:
          a. First offense:

          b. Subsequent offenses:

    B. Disorderly conduct (647(a)):

       1. Soliciting or engaging in _____ conduct in a _____ place/ (647(a) PC):

XII. Registration and notification sections:
    A. Sex offender registration (290 PC):
       1. Requirements:

       2. Crimes covered:

3. Publicizing offender statutes (290(m)(1) PC):

4. Penalty:

B. Notifications of arrest of school employees (291 and 291.1 PC):

Reading Assignment

1. California Penal Code Sections: 234.4, 261 – 264, 268 – 269b, 281 – 288a, 289, 290, 291, 291.1, 291.5, 314, 359, 647.6, 647(a).

Definitions

Define or explain the following:

A. Rape:

B. Unlawful intercourse:

C. Forcible rape:

D. Incest:

E. Fornication:

F. Sodomy:

G. Bestiality:

H. Child molesting:

I. Bigamy:

Problem exercise

1. Explain the seven forms of rape:

   a.

   b.

   c.

   d.

   e.

   f.

   g.

2. What are the prohibited relationships in incest?

3. Under what conditions is an act of oral copulation unlawful?

4. How long must a spouse be missing for the remaining spouse to marry without danger of bigamy?

5. When is sodomy a crime?

6. What is the maximum penalty for forcible rape?

7. What intent is necessary in felony child molesting?

8. Explain "unlawful intercourse" (261.5 PC).

   a. What defense may be used in this crime?

9. Briefly describe the sex offender registration and notification laws.

10. Explain the difference between misdemeanor and felony child molesting:

Chapter 15

Arson and Related Crimes

Introduction

Most of the specific crimes, which have been discussed thus far, are generally referred to as "crimes against person" because they involve personal injury to the victim. This includes crimes such as battery, homicide, sex offenses, kidnapping and assaults.

A second large classification of crimes is those offenses in which the victim's property is endangered. Included in this category are crimes such as theft, burglary, etc. These are called "crimes against property."

The crime of arson is a good bridge between these two general classifications of crimes because it involves elements of being both a crime against property and a crime against persons.

Arson is considered to be close to murder in seriousness because of the danger to human life which it creates.

There are two Penal Code Sections related to the burning of property. Both are often loosely referred to as "arson;" but only one of them is legally considered to be an arson; the other is simply referred to as unlawful burning.

Objectives

Upon completing this chapter you should be able to describe in detail the laws relating to arson, the burning of real and personal property, destroying insured real property and other related offenses.

Lecture Notes Outline

I. General Introduction:
   A. Two general penal code sections on arson and burning:
      1. 451 PC (Arson):

      2. 452 PC (Burning):

II. Definitions:
   A. Burn or burning:

   B. Willful (7 PC):

   C. Malicious (7 and 450 PC):

   D. Reckless (450 PC):

   E. Inhabited Structure:

   F. Uninhabited Structure:

III. Arson and burning code sections and penalties.

	Arson (451 PC)	Burning (452 PC)
Type of Damage or Injury caused:	**Specific Intent** Willful and malicious (deliberate, intentional)	**General Intent** Reckless – caused through negligence
With _____ _____ _____. _____ structure. (includes buildings within the "curtilage")	F – 5, 7 or 9 yrs. F – 3, 5 or 8 yrs.	F – 2, 4 or 6 yrs. F – 2, 3 or 4 yrs. M – 1yr.
_____ structure or	F – 2, 4 or 6 yrs.	F – 16 mos., 2 or 3 yrs M – 6 mos.
Other Real or Personal Property of _____ .	F – 16 mos., 2 or 3 yrs.	M – 6 mos.

** Definition of "Curtilage":

A. Penalty during a state of emergency (454 PC):

B. Additional penalty if arson is for financial gain (456 PC):

C. Penalty for death caused during an arson (187 & 190.2(17)(viii) PC):

IV. Related Crimes:
    A. Attempted Arson (455 PC):

        1. Covers burning under _____ only.

        2. General attempts:

        3. Punishment:

    B. False Fire Alarm (148.4 PC):

    C. Possession of fire bombs (453 PC):

    D. Arson Offender Registration law (457.1 PC):

Reading Assignment

1. California Penal Code: 7, 450 – 457.1, 148.4

Definitions

Define or explain the following:

A. Arson:

B. Curtilage:

C. Willful:

D. Malicious:

E. Reckless:

Problem Exercises

1. Under the "felony murder rule" what form of "arson" is intended under the "BARRM" felonies?

2. What amount of burning is necessary in every arson and burning crime?

3. What intent must exist in arson and burning crimes?

   a. Arson (451 PC):

   b. Burning (452 PC):

4. Compare attempt arson under 451a PC with other general attempts under 664 PC.

5. You are using a blowtorch and gasoline to remove paint from the side of your house when the house accidentally catches fire. There is approximately $4,000 damage before you can get it out, and it burns down your neighbor's garage. What crimes have you committed, if any, and what penalty?

6. You are using a blowtorch to remove paint from the side of your house when you decide to frighten your mother-in-law, who has been living in the back bedroom for the last seven years. You permit the wood under her window to catch fire while you are removing the paint. This causes some flame and smoke but you blow it out immediately. Your mother-in-law does not see what has happened and is not aware of it. What crimes have you committed, if any, and what penalty?

7. You are removing the paint form the side of your house using a blowtorch when you decide to frighten your mother-in-law into leaving, since she has been camped in your back bedroom for six months after coming for a weekend visit. You set a small pile of oily rags on the ground outside of her window. When she sees the smoke, she screams, calls the fire department and leaves, never to return. What crimes have you committed, if any, and what penalty?

Chapter 16

Theft and Forgery

Introduction

Stealing has always been the most common major crime. Ever since man developed the idea of owning something, there was someone else who wanted to take it away from him. Virtually every man, woman and child in America has been the victim of a theft at some time during their lives. Each year there are over five million thefts in this country; one approximately every ten seconds.

There are several types of theft, each having slightly different elements in the corpus delicti. Prior to 1927, each type was covered by a separate section of the Penal Code. At that time cases were lost if they were filed under the wrong section. Today, most forms of theft are included in just one section of the Penal Code, although it is still necessary to learn the distinctions between each type in order to determine if the necessary elements are present to establish the corpus delicti of any one of the several forms of theft. Forgery, a crime closely related to theft, is also examined in this chapter.

Objectives

Upon completing this chapter you should be able to give a detailed description of the various forms of the crime of theft, including larceny, theft by trick or device, theft by false pretenses, embezzlement and other related offenses, including the crime of forgery.

Lecture Notes Outline

I. Types of theft:

A.

B.   *484 PC*

C.

D.

II. Common elements in corpus delicti:

A. Actions of defendant:

B. Type of property:

C. Intent of victim in parting with property:

D. Intent of defendant in taking property:

III. Larceny (484 PC):

A. Elements:

1. Taking and carrying away

2. Personal property of another

3. Without their consent

4. With the intent to permanently deprive the owner of the property.

B. Analysis of Elements:

1. Act of defendant:

   a. _____ and _____

   Legally called:

   _____ and _____

   b. Requires:

   (1)

   And

   (2)

c. Examples:
    (1) Suitcase:

    (2) Overcoat:

    (3) Earrings:

2. Type of property:
    a. Definitions of property:

        (1)

        (2)

    b. Larceny includes only:

        P_____ P_____ of A_____

    c. Examples:

    d. Severed real property (487b and 487c PC):

e. Value of property:

f. Ownership of property:

3. Intent of victim:

4. Intent of defendant:

   a. Intent to _____
   _____.

   b. Borrowing temporarily:

      (1) Joyriding (499b PC & 10811 VC):

   c. Theft not for personal gain:

   d. Mistake:

e. Mistaken delivery:

C. Shoplifting (490.5 PC):
　　1. Definition:

　　2. Special provisions:

IV. Theft by false pretenses (484 PC): (_____)
　　A. Act of defendant:
　　　　1. Type of act:

　　　　2. Statements and Conduct not considered to be false:

　　B. Type of property:

　　　　1.

　　　　2. Usually _____

C. Intent of victim:

    1. Transfer _____ to _____.

    2. Reliance:

D. Intent and knowledge of defendant:
    1. Permanently deprive owner of property (same as larceny):

    2. _____ of the _____ :

E. Corroboration (532b PC):

F. Related Crimes:
    1. Defrauding an innkeeper (537 PC):

    2. Other:

V. Theft by trick and device (484 PC):
    A. Act of defendant:
        1. Similar to _____

        2. Frequently called: _____

3. Defendant uses a _____

4. Examples:

B. Type of property:
  1. Same as in theft by false pretenses (real or personal):

C. Intent of victim:

D. Intent of defendant:
  1. Same as theft by false pretenses (intent to permanently deprive owner of property and has knowledge of falsehoods).

VI. Embezzlement (503 – 514 PC):
  A. Act of defendant:

B. Relationship of defendant to victim:
   1. Fiduciary relationship:

      a. Embezzlement by public officials (424 PC):

      b. Vehicle dealers and rental companies (10855 VC):

C. Type of property:
   1. Same as theft by false pretenses (real or personal):

D. Intent of victim:

E. Intent of defendant (512 PC):

   1. Comparison with other types of theft:

VII. Degrees of theft:
   A. Grand theft (optional felony – 487 PC):
      1. Based on value:

         a. Over $_____ (fair market value):

         (1) Employee theft:

b. Over $ _____ if property stolen is:

    (1)

    (2)

    (3)

2. Place from which stolen:

3. Type of property:

4. Penalty for grand theft (489 PC):

    a. Special Enhancements (12022.6 and 12022.7 PC):

B. All other is petty theft (misdemeanor – 488 PC):
  1. Penalty for petty theft (490 PC):

    a. With priors (666 PC):

VIII. Crimes related to theft:
    A. Theft, forgery or fraudulent use of credit cards (484d to 484j PC):

    B. Theft of lost property (485 PC):

    C. Joyriding (499b – 499d PC, 10851 VC):

        1. Vehicle types:

    D. Defrauding telephone company (502.7 PC):

    E. Use of slugs in coin operated machines and phones (640a and 640b PC):

    F. Unauthorized connection to cable TV (593d PC):

G. Use or sale of unauthorized (pirated) recorded material (653h PC):

H. Computer fraud (502 PC):

    1. Theft (pirating) computer programs (499c PC):

IX. Forgery and related crimes:
    A. Forgery (470 PC):
        1. Elements:
            a. Types of acts prohibited:

            b. Types of documents which can be forged:

            c. Intent:

2. Penalty (473 PC):

B. Non-sufficient fund "N.S.F." checks (476a PC):
   1. Elements:

      a.

      b.

      c.

   2. Analysis:
      a. Knowledge:

      b. Intent:

   3. Penalty:
      a. Over $450.00:

      b. Under $450.00:

      c. Civil penalty:

C. Related crimes:

   1. Issuing check on nonexistent bank (476 PC):

   2. Falsifying I.D. or driver's license with intent to use in forgery or N.S.F. (470 a and b PC):

   3. Forgery of government or corporation seals (472 PC):

   4. Sending false phone or telegraph message (474 PC):

   5. Using name of another in writing to a newspaper (538a PC):

6. Falsifying, stealing, removing or destroying public records (court, land, tax records, etc.) (6200 to 6201 Government Code):

7. Forging prescriptions (4390 Bus. And Prof. Code):

8. Trademark forgeries (14320 to 14321 B and P Code):

9. Election forgeries (14691 and 29100 to 29102 Election Code):

Reading Assignment

1. California Penal Code Sections: 72, 332, 424, 470 to 476a, 481, 484, 484d to 484j, 485, 487, 487a, b, c, d, e, f, g, 488, 489, 490.5, 491, 492, 498, 499, 499a, b, c, d, 502.7, 503, 514, 537, 538a, 593d, e, 640a, b, 653h, 666, 12022.6

Definitions

Define or explain the following:

A. Theft:

B. Larceny:

C. Theft by false pretenses:

D. Theft by trick and device:

E. Embezzlement:

F. Caption and asportation:

G. Personal property:

H. Real property:

I. Fiduciary position:

J. Joyriding:

K. Fair market value:

L. Bunco:

M. Grand theft:

N. Petty theft:

16-13

O. Forgery:

P. N.S.F.:

Chapter Problems

1. R. M. Rath and C. S. Pecht work in the same office together. Rath forgets and leaves his watch on his desk when he leaves work one evening. Pecht decides to take it with him in order to safeguard it. Later that evening, Pecht is in a restaurant with a girl and finds that he doesn't have enough money to pay the check. He sells Rath's watch to the waiter in order to pay his bill. What crimes have been committed, if any?

2. Paul has his hubcaps stolen by Carl. Learning that Carl stole the hubcaps, Paul goes to Carl's house to get them back. Carl is not home. He can't find them, but does see a set of chrome valve covers which will fit his car and which he knows Carl and John had stolen from Stanley. Paul takes the valve covers to make up for the hubcaps which were stolen form him. Carl later accuses Paul of theft for taking the covers. Is Carl right?

3. Pat and Mike are members of the same church. Pat was selling church raffle tickets for a new car at three for a dollar. Mike agreed to buy three tickets. Pat mistakenly count out four tickets instead of three. Mike sees the error but says nothing. Make takes the tickets and gets about ten feet away when Pat discovers the error and calls him back. Mike refuses to return the extra ticket and Pat calls the police. What crimes have been committed, if any?

4. Slicker Sam runs a used car lot. He gets in a car with a broken block and a bad transmission. Joe comes in to buy a car and is shown the wreck. Joe asks how it runs and Sam says, "It's the best one in town," even though he knows about the bad motor and transmission. Joe asks if the engine is in good shape and Sam says that their mechanic has just looked it over and that the engine is in top shape with absolutely nothing wrong with it. Joe sees the crack in the block but figures that he can fix it up with no trouble by pouring in a can of Stop-Leak. Joe buys the car and three days later the transmission drops out and the engine blows up. Joe calls the police department and complains. What crimes have been committed, if any?

5. Complete the following chart showing a comparison of the corpus delicti elements of the various types of theft:

	Larceny	False Pretenses	Trick or Device	Embezzlement
Act of Defendant:				
Type of Property:				
Intent of Victim:				
Intent of Defendant:				

Chapter 17

Robbery

Introduction

Robbery is one of the crimes which has the combined characteristics of being both a crime against persons and a crime against property. One of the elements of every robbery is that a theft must occur. Some property must be stolen. Thus robbery may be classified as a crime against property. It is also true that every robbery must include a direct face-to-face contact between the criminal and his victim. Therefore it may also be considered a crime against the person. It is because of this direct contact between robber and the victim, that robbery is considered to be one of the most dangerous of crimes. There is always the possibility of death or serious injury. Unfortunately, robbery is growing in frequency and is becoming more prevalent among juveniles. Many tragedies have occurred, for both victims and thieves, when the juvenile criminal loses his bravado, panics and attacks the victim. This can easily result in the death of either party.

Objectives

Upon completing this chapter you should be able to completely explain the laws relating to the crime of robbery and briefly describe other related crimes such as extortion and car highjacking.

Lecture Notes Outline

I. Elements (211 PC):

   A.

   B.

   C.

II. Analysis:
    A. Felonious taking of personal property:
        1. Includes all elements of _____

           a.

           b.

           c.

    B. From the person or immediate presence of victim:

        1. Forcing victim to leave:

    C. By us of force *or* fear:
        1. Force:

        2. Fear:

3. Purpose of force or fear:

III. Degrees of robbery (212.5 PC):
  A. First degree:

  B. Second degree:

IV. Penalties (213 PC):
  A. First degree:

  B. Second degree:

  C. Common enhancement factors:
    1. Weapons:

      a. _____ with _____ (12022 PC):

        (1) Meaning of "armed":

        (2) Added penalty:

        (3) Liability of co-principals:

      b. _____ of _____ (12022.5 PC):

        (1) Meaning of "use":

        (2) Added penalty:

c. _____ of _____ other than a firearm (12022 PC):

   (1) Type of weapons:

   (2) Additional penalty:

d. Theory of weapons enhancements:
   (1) Rationale:

   (2) Victim Unaware:

   (3) Simulated gun:

   (4) Unloaded gun:

   (5) Toy gun:

2. Causing _____ (12022.7 PC):

   a. Added penalty:

3. Value of stolen property (12022.6 PC):

   a. Over $65,000:

   b. Over $200,000:

   c. Over $1,300,000:

   d. Over $3,200,000:

4. Prior convictions:

V. Car Jacking (215 PC):
   A. Elements:

   B. Penalty:

VI. Extortion (518 PC):
   Also called _____ .

   A. Description:

   B. Comparison to robbery:

   C. Penalty:

Reading Assignment

1. California Penal Code Sections: 518 – 524 briefly, 211 – 215

Definitions

Define or explain the following:
A. Robbery:

B. First degree robbery:

C. Armed:

D. Use of a deadly or dangerous weapon:

E. Extortion:

Chapter Problems

In the following problems, determine whether a robbery has been committed and if so what penalty enhancements apply. If a robbery has not been committed, determine if any other crime has occurred.

1. Ira Ballpoint walks into his local liquor store and, jabbing his finger into his coat pocket so as to simulate a gun, walks up to Henry the clerk and says "Gimme your dough." Ira intends to steal the money from the cash register but Henry, thinking it is all a joke, merely laughs at him. Ira becomes flustered, grabs some change from the counter, and runs out of the store.

2. Harry Quagmire loans his bicycle pump to his next-door neighbor, Charlie. After three weeks Charlie has not returned the pump. This irritates Harry so he gets his .22 cal. rifle, loads it, and goes next door. He meets Charlie in the garage and demands the bicycle pump. The sight of the gun scares Charlie out of his wits and he gives Harry the pump.

3. Irving took Martha to a movie and, while driving home, parks in a secluded area, leans over, and says "How about a goodnight kiss, sweetie?" This so scares Martha that she jumps out of the car and runs to her house. Irving then finds that she has left her purse in the car. He opens it and steals a two-dollar bill, the only money in the purse.

4. Mary works for a drug store and is given the task of taking the day's receipts to the bank. She carries the money in a plain paper sack under he left arm. While she is enroute to the bank, Felonious Phil walks up behind her and snatches the bag from her before she realizes what has happened. He runs down the street with the sack containing $450.00 while Mary screams that she has been robbed.

5. Charlie gets into a poker game with three people, one of whom is a stranger to the group. As the game progresses, it becomes obvious that the stranger is winning more than any of the others. After losing about $25.00, Charlie becomes suspicious and examines the cards. He finds that they are marked and that the stranger has been cheating in the game. Charlie pulls out a knife, points it at the stranger, and demands his money back. The stranger, fearful of being stabbed, returns to Charlie the amount which Charlie lost.

6. Hiram walks into Pete's grocery store with an unloaded gun in his back pocket and tells Pete to hand over the money in the cash register. Hiram is much larger than Pete and Pete gives him the money because he is afraid of being beaten if he refuses. Pete never sees or knows about the gun.

7. Hiram walks into Pete's store and points a lightweight plastic toy pistol at Pete. Pete believes it is a real gun and is scared out of his wits. Hiram demands the money in the register and Pete gives it to him.

5. Charlie gets into a poker game with three people, one of whom is a stranger to the group. As the game progresses, it becomes obvious that the stranger is winning more than any of the others. After losing about $25.00, Charlie becomes suspicious and examines the cards. He finds that they are marked and that the stranger has been cheating in the game. Charlie pulls out a knife, points it at the stranger and demands his money back. The stranger, fearing of being stabbed, returns to Charlie the amount which Charlie lost.

6. Juan walks into Pete's grocery store with an unloaded gun in his back pocket and over the money in the cash register. Blinda is much larger than Pete and Pete gives Juan the money because he is afraid of being beaten or robbed. Pete never sees or knows about the gun.

7. Juan walks into Pete's store and points a lightweight plastic toy gun at him. Pete, believing it is loaded and in fear of his own life, empties the register and Pete gives it to him.

Chapter 18

Burglary and Receiving Stolen Property

Introduction

The crime of burglary has existed from the very earliest common law. The word itself is derived from two Anglo-Saxon words: *burgh*, meaning *home;* and *laran*, meaning *thief;* thus – *burg-laran* or *home thief.* Under common law, only a home could be subject to burglary.

Although burglary exists as a crime in some form in every state, the name given to it and the specific elements required for its violation vary somewhat across the country. You may find basically the same act referred to as "breaking and entering," "aggravated larceny," "felonious trespass," or some other similar term. In California, they are all encompassed in the crime called burglary.

Objectives

Upon completing this chapter you should be able to describe all of the elements of the crimes of burglary and receiving stolen property and briefly explain related laws such as burglary with explosives, possession of burglary tools and the liability of second hand dealers.

Lecture Notes Outline

I. Burglary (459 PC):

   A. Introduction:

   B. Corpus delicti:

      1.

      2.

      3.

C. Analysis:
   1. Intent – most important element:
      a. Intent to Commit _____ or_____ .

      b. Timing of intent:

      c. Proof of intent:

      d. Completion of intended theft or felony:

   2. Entry:
      a. Breaking as an element:

         (1) Common law:

      b. Lawful entry:

c. Methods of entry:

d. Completion of burglary:

    (1) Apartment and office buildings:

3. Place entered:
   a. Building:
    (1) Must have_____ and _____.

    (2) General Examples:

    (3) Building under construction:

    (4) Size:

   b. Mines, caves, boats, railroad cars, airplanes, trailers, tents:

c. Automobiles:

d. Cargo containers (458 PC):

D. Degrees of burglary (460 PC):
   1. First degree:
      a. Burglary of: _____

         (1) Inhabited:
             (a) General:

             (b) Vacation dwelling:

             (c) New construction:

             (d) Vessels:

   2. Second degree:

E. Penalties (461 PC):
   1. First degree:

   2. Second degree:

F. Common enhancements:
    1. Armed with a deadly weapon (12022 PC):

    2. Inflicting serious injury (12022.7 PC):

    3. Value of property stolen (12022.6 PC):
       a. Over $65,000:

       b. Over $200,000:

       c. Over $1,300,000:

       d. Over $3,200,000:

    4. Prior convictions:

II. Burglary with explosives (464 PC):
  A. Elements:

    1.

    2.

    3.

    4.

    5.

  B. Penalty:

  C. Note:

III. Possession of burglary tools (466 PC):
   A. Forms of crime:

      1.

      2.

      3.

   B. Type of tool:

   C. Intent:

   D. Penalty:

   E. Related crimes:

      1. Possession of keys or tools to open coin-operated machines (466.3 PC):

      2. Unauthorized possession of vehicle master keys (466.5 PC):

      3. Unauthorized possession or duplication of public building keys (469 PC):

IV. Receiving stolen property (496 PC):
   A. Elements:

      1.

      2.

      3.

   B. Analysis:
      1. Buying or receiving:

2. Type of property:

3. Knowledge:
    a. Test:

    b. Evidence of knowledge:

    c. Legal presumptions of knowledge (496 PC):

4. Fraud:

C. Penalty:

D. Title to property:

V. Crimes related to receiving stolen property:
   A. Purchase of wire, books, etc. (496a – 496b PC):

   B. Purchase or sale of article with altered I.D. number (537e PC):

Reading Assignment

1. California Penal Code Sections: 458 –466, 466.3, 466.5, 469, 496, 496a, 496b, 537e.

Definitions

Define or explain the following:

A. Burgh:

B. Laran:

C. Entry (as used in burglary):

D. Building (as used in burglary):

E. Explosive (as used in 464 PC):

F. Receiving stolen property:

G. Burglary tools (as used in 466 PC):

H. Common law burglary:

Chapter Problems

In the following problems, discuss the criminal liability of each party, if any. If a crime or crimes have been committed, determine at what moment each crime was legally complete.

1. Sal and Sue go into the Broadway Department store intending to steal a watch. They walk through the jewelry department but find nothing available. Finding that they will be unable to steal a watch, they decide to do some shopping and go to the third floor ladies wear department. Sal has $3.00 and intends to buy a blouse but she sees a sweater for $16.00. She slips the sweater under the blouse she is wearing and, taking Sue by the arm, walks out of the dress department, down the escalator to the street and out the front door. Once outside in the parking lot she unbuttons her blouse and removes the sweater. Sue is surprised to see this as she had not seen Sal take the sweater. Sal gives the sweater to Sue and asks her to put in her large handbag so that they can walk past the parking lot guard without his becoming suspicious. Sue carries the sweater to the car for her. Sal later discovers that the sweater is too small for her and she gives it to her younger sister, Anne, explaining that she bought it with some money she had earned babysitting.

2. Paul comes to Vince's wedding as a guest. As the wedding starts, Paul, who is out of work and broke, sees the wedding gifts in a side room and decides to steal some. He picks up two large packages and starts toward the door when he hears a shout. Fearing that he has been discovered, he drops the packages and runs. Actually, the shout is from a woman who has just entered the church and stopped the ceremony, claiming that she is Vincent's wife. Vince admits that she is his wife and says that he thought she was in Chicago and that he had not heard from her in six months. In the confusion which results, Paul sneaks back into the church hoping to get another chance at the presents. He walks out with several of the wedding gifts, including a watch, radio, silverware, record player and toaster. He sells it all except the silverware to a man named Henderson who he met on a bus a few days later. Henderson paid him about 20% of what the goods were worth. He gave the silverware back to the person who had originally sent it to Vince as a wedding present. This friend, named Carl, was happy to get it back as he was afraid Vincent would try to keep it after the wedding had been called off.

3. Joe gets a job with Sam's auto parts and proceeds to give his friends discounts not authorized by Sam. Sam has to be at Vince's wedding on Saturday so he puts Joe in charge of the store by himself. Joe tells his friend Phil to drop by the store on Saturday and that he'll "fix him up." Phil doesn't know what Joe means but he drops by anyway. Joe sells him a $75.00 set of wire rims for $8.00. Later the same day, Phil decides to get more out of Joe. He goes back to the store and tells Joe that he wants a $45.00 tune up kit for nothing or he will tell Sam about what Joe is doing. Joe agrees and gets the kit and gives it to Phil. Just then Sam comes back into the store because the wedding ceremony had ended a lot sooner than expected. He sees the transaction and nabs Phil before he gets out the door. He holds both Joe and Phil and calls the police.

Chapter 19

Crimes Against Governmental Institutions and Functions

Introduction

Most criminal statutes are designed to protect people from personal injury or loss of their property. They neatly fit into the classifications of "Crimes Against the Person" or "Crimes Against Property." An important characteristic of these crimes is that each has a specific victim who has suffered some loss or injury.

There is another category of crime in which there is no single identifiable victim. These offenses are commonly referred to as "victimless crimes," and include crimes such as narcotics, gambling and prostitution violations.

This chapter describes some crimes which do not readily fit into any of these categories. They are crimes which endanger society itself by jeopardizing the functions of government. They are "crimes against government institutions."

Some of these crimes, such as treason, threaten the very existence of a democratic government. Others, such as bribery and perjury, undermine the principles which form the foundations of governmental institutions such as the system of justice. All such institutions function on the propositions that:

Public officials will perform honestly;
Legislators will vote objectively;
Judges will decide fairly;
Jurors will deliberate honestly;
Witnesses will testify truthfully.

If these propositions are not true, then governmental integrity is lost and its very existence imperiled. The laws described in this chapter are intended to protect the institutions of government, particularly our system of justice.

Objectives

Upon completion of this chapter you should be able to do the following:

1. Describe the crime of treason.

2. Describe the elements of bribery.

3. Recognize the various statutes relating to bribery and be able to describe the difference between them.

4. Define and describe the crimes of perjury, subornation of perjury and soliciting perjury.

5. Explain contempt of court, including the difference between civil and criminal contempts and the t types of acts constituting contempt.

6. Define embracery.

7. Define barratry.

8. Briefly describe the statutes relating to the making of false police reports and of impersonating police.

Lecture Notes Outline

I. Treason (U.S. Constitution, Art. III Par. 3; Calif. Penal Code 37):
   A. Definition:

   B. Importance:

   C. Important elements:
      1. Violator must owe allegiance to U.S. government:

      2. What constitutes a treasonous act?

   D. Penalty for treason:

II. Bribery and related crimes:

    A. Elements (7[6] PC):

      1. _____ or _____ something of _____ ,

      2. with a _____ intent to _____ influence,

      3. the _____ , _____ or opinion of the person to whom it is given,

      4. in their _____ or _____ capacity.

    B. Analysis:
      1. "Thing of value":

      2. "Corrupt intent" (7[3] PC):

      3. Objective of bribe:

      4. Position of person receiving bribe:

C. Bribery statutes:
   1. General:

      a. Common format:

         (1) Types of acts prohibited:

         (2) Position or status of parties involved:

         (3) Objective to be achieved by the bribe:

         (4) Penalty:

   2. Specific bribery statutes:

      The chart starting on the next page lists all of the major California statutes relating to bribery. It is organized according to the common format of bribery statutes as described on the previous page.

      The chart has been deliberately left incomplete. In order to familiarize yourself with these sections you should locate each one in the Penal Code and read through it at least once. The following assignment is intended to help you accomplish this.

      ASSIGNMENT: Locate each code section listed on the chart, read it, and fill in the blank spaces on the chart. Note that each page of the chart is duplicated on the following page, which is designed as a written assignment sheet. This second page is to be removed from the book and submitted to your instructor as homework if requested.

	Code Section Number	Parties Who May Commit Act	Acts Prohibited by Statute	Parties to Whom Action Is Directed	Objective of the Bribe	Penalty
A. Bribery Statutes Affecting Public Employees	67 PC	Anyone	Giving or Offering a Bribe	Public Executive Officer	To Influence Any Act, Decision or Vote	2, 3 or 4 years &/or Disqualified to Hold Office
	67 ½ PC			Any State, County or City Employee	Not Specified	May Be A Misdemeanor or Felony
	68 PC	Any Executive, or Ministerial Officer or Employee of Govt.	Asking, Receiving or Agreeing to Receive a Bribe	From Anyone	Influence Any Act or Vote	
B. Bribery Statutes Affecting Elected Officials	85 PC	Anyone	Giving or Offering a Bribe		Influence Any Act, Decision or Vote	
	86 PC	State Legislator	Asking, Receiving or Agreeing to Receive a Bribe	From Anyone		2, 3 or 4 years Removal from Office, Disqualified to Hold Office and Loss of Voting Rights

	165 PC (first part)	Anyone	Giving or Offering a Bribe		Corruptly Influence Official Act	2, 3 or 4 years
	165 PC (second part)	City Councilman or County Board of Supervisors	Receiving or Offering or Agreeing to Receive a Bribe	From Anyone		2, 3 or 4 years, Removal from Office, Disqualification to Hold Office, Loss of Voting Rights
	Calif. Constitution, Art. IV, Sec. 35	Anyone	"Bribing"	Member of State Legislature	Not Specified	Felony (16 mos., 2yrs. or 3 years)
C. Bribery Statutes Affecting Judicial Officials	92 PC		Giving or Offering a Bribe	Judge, Juror, Referee, Commissioner or Other Judicial Office	Influence Vote or Decision	2, 3 or 4 years
	93 PC		Asking Receiving or Agreeing to Receive a Bribe	From Anyone		2, 3 or 4 years Removal from Office, Disqualification to Hold Office (per 98 PC)

D. Bribery Statutes Affecting Court Witnesses	136 ½ PC	Anyone	Giving or Offering	Court Witness		Felony
	137 PC				Influence Testimony	Felony
	138 PC	Court Witness	Receiving or Offering to Receive a Bribe	From Anyone	Influence Testimony or Refrain from Testifying	Felony

E. Bribery Statutes Affecting Sporting Events	It should be noted that the following sections do not apply to professional wrestling exhibitions (18607 Business and Professions Code).					
	337b PC	Anyone	Giving, Offering or Attempting to Give or Offer a Bribe		Refrain from Using Best Efforts to Win or Attempt to Limit the Margin of Victory	16 mos., 2 yrs. or 3 years
	337c PC	Player	Accepting, or Offering or Agreeing to Accept a Bribe	From Anyone		
	337d PC	Anyone	Giving, Offering or Attempting to Give or Offer a Bribe		Corruptly Influence Results of Event	
	337e PC	Umpire, Referee, Manager or Other Official	Accepting, or Offering or Agreeing to Accept a Bribe	From Anyone		

F. Bribery Statutes Affecting Elections	Election Code Sections: 12000 to 12012 and 29160	Anyone	Giving, Offering, Receiving or Agreeing to Give, Offer or Receive Any Money, Gift, Loan or Other Valuable Including Employment	Anyone	Voting or Not Voting; Voting or Not Voting for a Particular Candidate or Question. Voting Against a Particular Candidate, Withdrawing Candidacy. Going or Not Going to Polls. Affecting Nomination of Candidate at Convention. Inducing Another to Do Any of the Above	Felony, 16 mos., 2 yrs. or 3 years

3. Commercial Bribery (641.3 PC):
   a. Description:

   b. Penalty:

4. Crimes related to bribery:
   a. Influencing officials by intimidation or threat:
      (1) Threatening public employees (71 PC):

      (2) Threatening court witnesses (137 PC):

b. Public officials accepting rewards, gratuities or fees other than the authorized fees or salaries for performing official services:

(1) 70 PC: Any public official accepting a reward, gratuity or fee for performing official duties:

(2) 70.5 PC: _____ Commissioner charging a fee other than

authorize for performing _____ .

(3) 94.5 PC: Judge accepting any fee or gratuity whatever for performing

_____ , other than the fee expressly provided by law.

(4) 73 PC: Buying appointment to a public position.

(5) 74 PC: Selling appointments or deputization.

(a) Penalty:

(6) 94 PC: _____ accepting gratuity or reward for performing official acts.

c. Legislative vote swapping (86 PC):

III. Crimes against judicial process:
A. Perjury and related crimes:
1. Definition and elements of perjury (118, 118a PC; 2015.5 CCP; 1368, 3108 Govt. Code; 11054, 12103 and 12850 WIC):

a. "A false statement or writing . . .

b. . . . concerning some material fact . . .

c. . . . made under oath . . .

d. . . . with knowledge that it is a falsehood."

2. Statute of Limitations:

3. Penalty for perjury (126, 128 PC):

4. Subornation and soliciting of perjury:
   a. Soliciting (653f PC):

   b. Subornation (127 PC):

5. Corroboration (653f and 1103a PC):

6. Falsifying evidence (132 to 135 PC):

B. Offenses against trial proceedings:
　　1. Contempt of court (166 PC):
　　　　a. Introduction:

　　　　b. Civil contempt:

　　　　c. Criminal contempt (166 PC):

　　　　d. Contempt proceedings:

　　　　e. Other forms of contempt:

　　2. Embracery (95 to 96 PC):

　　3. Picketing Court House (169 PC):

4. Invading Privacy of Jury (167 PC):

5. Other Related Sections:
   a. 116 and 117 PC:

   b. 136 PC:

   c. 136 ½, 137 and 138 PC:

C. Offenses against grand jury proceedings (924 to 924.3 PC):

D. Barratry (158 to 159 PC):

IV. Crimes obstructing government emergency services and personnel:
   A. False reports:
      1. Introduction:

      2. Specific Statutes:

         a. False report of an emergency (148.3 PC):

b. False fire alarms (148.4 PC):

c. False bomb reports (148.1 PC):

d. False crime reports (148.5 PC):

e. Peace officer submitting false report (6204 Govt. Code):

B. Impersonating police officer or firefighter:
   1. 146a PC:

   2. 146b PC:

   3. 146c PC:

   4. 538d and 538e PC:

C. Use of business card or other device to gain immunity from enforcement of law (146d PC):

D. Police phone numbers and addresses (146e PC):

E. Other related sections:
    1. Resisting Arrest (148, 148.2 & 69 PC):
        a. Elements:
            (1) Willful resistance, delay or obstruction . . .

            (2) . . . Of a public official . . .

            (3) . . . In the performance of their duties.

        b. Penalty:

    2. Refusing to aid a peace officer (Posse Comitatus) (150 PC):

    3. Advocating and inciting others to unlawfully injure or kill a peace officer (151 PC):

Reading Assignment

1. California Penal Code Sections: 7(3), 7(6),37, 67, 67 ½, 68, 70, 70.5, 71, 73, 74, 85, 86, 92, 93, 94, 94.5, 95, 96, 98, 116, 117, 118, 118a, 121, 123, 125, 126, 127, 128, 132 – 135, 148.1, 148.3, 148.4, 148.5, 146a, b, c, d and e, 148, 150, 151, 158, 159, 165, 166, 167, 169, 337b, c, d and e, 538d and e, 641.3, 653f, 924, 924.1, .2, and .3, 1103a

Definitions

Define or explain the following:

A. Treason:

B. Misprision of treason:

C. Sedition:

D. Bribery:

E. Corrupt:

F. Perjury:

G. Subornation of perjury:

H. Embracery:

I. Barratry:

Chapter 20

Crimes Against Public Peace
and Order

Introduction

One theory of political philosophy holds that government has an implied contract with the taxpayers. The government agrees to perform certain functions and provide certain protection, in return for which the citizen agrees to support the government and pay taxes. Part of this agreement is a guarantee that citizens will be protected from disturbing, riotous or offensive conduct and that order will be maintained in the community. This chapter is devoted to a study of the laws designed to fulfill this guarantee.

Some of these laws are commonly and routinely enforce by police agencies as part of their duty to maintain order. In carrying out this function a disproportionately large amount of police effort has sometimes been devoted to relatively minor violations. Efforts are now underway to redefine the police role in this field. This is particularly true of drunk laws, which account for over 50% of all arrest activity in some jurisdictions; a rate which many authorities feel is a misdirected use of police resources.

Some of these laws are not being redesigned with an emphasis on the preventative rather than the punitive goals. In order to reduce law enforcement and judicial involvement, police are being encouraged to develop conflict resolution techniques which will decrease the incidence of legal action. Disturbing the peace is an example of this type of crime; in which police action is more frequently taking the form of warning and advice rather than arrest.

Other crimes examined in this chapter provide a challenge to an officer's legal and professional skills because of the unique circumstances under which they arise. Crimes such as rioting, unlawful assembly and other acts of mob violence, although less frequent than drunk arrests, pose a far greater threat to the peace and safety of the community. If sufficiently aggravated they may even warrant the mobilization of the military power of the state. Enforcement of these laws also provides a ready arena for conflict with the First Amendment constitutional rights to freedom of speech and assembly. If mishandled, they may open the door to charges of civil rights violations.

For these reasons, you should take particular care to understand the limitations and application of the statutes examined in this chapter.

Objectives

Upon the completion of this chapter, you should be able to do the following:

1. Fully describe the elements of public drunkenness and explain the civil protective custody and d detoxification procedures applicable to drunk arrests.
2. List and describe the most common California statutes relating to the care of animals.

3. Fully explain the crime of disturbing the peace, including the elements and enforcement policies.
4. Describe the California criminal statutes pertaining to school disturbances and the Penal Code Sections prohibiting unlawful entry to school grounds.
5. Define and explain the differences between riot, rout, rescue, lynching and inciting to riot.
6. Full describe the elements of unlawful assembly and explain the requirements and procedures for enforcing dispersal orders, including constitutional conflicts.
7. Briefly describe the California Emergency Services Act in relation to civil disturbances and the declaration of martial law.
8. Briefly describe the California statutes relating to:

   a. Obstructing sidewalks.
   b. Making obscene phone calls.
   c. Party crashing.
   d. Begging.
   e. Disturbing public meetings.

Lecture Notes Outline

I. Offensive conduct:
   A. Introduction:

   B. Specific offenses:
      1 Public Drunkenness (647f PC):
         a. Elements:
            (1) Condition:
                Under the influence to the extent that:

                (a)

                   or

                (b)

      2. Location:

(3) Substances:

b. Treatment provisions (647g PC):
   (1) Background:

   (2) Procedure:

   c. Penalty:

2. Begging (647 (c) PC):
   a. Act:

   b. Location:

   c. Purpose:

3. Obstructing street or sidewalk (647 c PC):
   (Do not confuse section numbers.)

   a. Willfully and maliciously . . .

   b. Obstruct _____ . . .

c. Along any _____ .

4. Offensive phone calls (653m PC):

5. Crimes against animals (596 –599e PC):

   a. Poisoning (596 PC):

   b. Cruelty to animals (597, 597a, 597e and 597f PC):

      (1) Acts prohibited:

      (2) Penalty:

   c. Fighting animals (597, 597b, 597c, 597i, 597j, 597m PC):

   d. Authority to provide care for or kill animal (597e and 597f PC):

e. Abandonment of dogs and cats (597s PC):

f. Using pet animals for food (598b PC):

g. Agitating, injuring or killing police animal (600 PC):

II. General disturbances:

A. Introduction:

B. Specific statutes:

1. Disturbing the peace (415 PC):

   a. Forms of crime:

      (1) Unlawfully _____ in a _____

      _____ or _____ another to _____ .:

      (2) Disturbing _____ _____ by

      _____ and _____ _____ .:

(3) Using _____ _____ in a

_____ _____ which tend to invite an

_____ _____ of the _____ .

    b. Penalty:

2. Loud vehicle sound systems (27007 VC):

3. Displaying weapons (417 PC):

4. Disturbing meetings:

    a. 302 PC:

    b. 12046 and 29440 Elections Code:

    c. 403 PC:

5. Party crashing (602.5 PC):

III. School disturbances:
    A. Introduction:

B. Specific statutes:

1. Disturbances on college campuses (415.5 PC):

    a. Where applicable:

    b. Act (same as 415 PC):

        (1)

            or

        (2)
            or

        (3)

    c. Penalty:

2. Obstructing access to college campuses (602.10 PC):

    a. Where applicable:

    b. Prohibited act:

    c. Intent:

    d. Penalty:

3. Statutes relating to trespassing on schools or colleges:

Penal Code Section	Applicable to:	Where Applicable:	Prohibited Act:	Additional Elements:
626.2	Students or Employees	Public Colleges, Universities, High Schools, Jr. High Schools and Elementary Schools	Entering After _____ or _____	None
626.4	Any Person	Same as above	Remaining on or Entering After Right to Enter Has Been Revoked	1. Must have _____ to believe person has _____ 2. Revocation valid for _____ days.
626.6	Persons Other Than Students or Employees	Same as above	Remaining on or Entering Within _____ After Being Directed to Leave.	1. Person must be _____ act likely to _____ or must have _____
626.8	Any Person	Same as above	Same as above	Mere _____ is sufficient if it tends to disrupt.

4. Possession of firearms or knives on school or college grounds (626.9 and 626.10 PC):

    a. Where applicable:

    b. Type of weapons:

    c. Confiscation:

5. Loitering near schools and playgrounds without lawful business (653g PC):

IV. Mob violence, unlawful assembly and related crimes:

A. Historical background:

B. Constitutional conflicts:

C. Specific statutes relating to mob violence:

    1. Riot (404 PC):

        a. Elements:

            (1) _____ acting together . . .

(2) . . . Who use any _____ or _____ ,

disturbing the _____ peace . . .

(3) . . . *OR*, who _____ such force or violence, having the

_____.

b. Penalty:

2. Inciting to riot (404.6 PC):

   a. Elements:

      (1) _____ others to riot or commit acts of violence . . .

      (2) . . . with the _____ to cause a riot or violence . . .

      (3) . . . and where there is a _____ and _____ danger that such
      riot or violence will result:

   b. Analysis:
   (1) First Amendment conflicts:

   (2) Intent:

(3) "Clear and present danger":

c. Enforcement difficulties:

d. Penalty:

D. Unlawful assemblies and related crimes:
   1. Unlawful assembly (407, 408 PC):
      a. Purpose:

      b. Elements:

         (1) _____ persons, assembled together . . .

            (a) advance agreement _____ necessary.

         (2) . . . to commit an _____ act . . .

            (a) Type of act:

            (b) Completion of intended crimes:

            (c) Proof of intent or likelihood:

(3) . . . or commit a _____ act in a violent manner.

      (a) Common example:

  b. Penalty:

2. Refusing to leave a public building (602 [p] PC):
  a. Elements:

    (1) Refusing to leave a _____ building . . .

    (2) . . . during hours when the building is _____ to the _____ . . .

    (3) . . . when requested to do so by _____ or _____ . . .

    (4) . . . if surrounding circumstances indicate that the person has _____

    _____ _____ _____ .

  b. Applicability:

  c. Order to leave:

  d. Penalty:

  e. Trespassing in state capitol (171f PC):

3. Dispersal of unlawful assemblies:
  a. Responsibility and authority of police (410, 723, 726,727 PC):

b. Statutes authorizing dispersal:

(1) 409 PC: _____ remaining present at the scene of
_____ after being ordered to leave.

(a) Applicable to:

(b) Purpose of section:

(2) 416 PC: _____ assembled for the purpose of
_____ or _____.
who do not disperse on command of officers.

(a) Applicable to:

(b) Restitution:

c. Dispersal order (726 PC):

(1) When required:

(2) Who may give:

(3) Form of order:

(a)

(b)

(c)

(d)

(e)

(4) Proof of hearing order:

4. Psychology of riots:

5. Crimes related to unlawful assembly:

   a. Lynching (405a PC):

   b. Rescue (4550 PC):

   c. Resisting arrest, interfering or obstructing justice (148, 69 PC):

   d. Advocating killing or injury of a peace officer (151 PC):

   e. Blocking sidewalks (647c PC):

   f. Throwing, dispensing or depositing any offensive substances in public assembly (375 PC):

E. Entering any location for the purpose of causing damage or interfering with lawful business (602 [j] PC):

   1. Elements:

      a. "Willfully entering" . . .

      b. . . . "any lands" . . .

         (1) includes::

      c. . . . "for the purpose of injuring property or property rights" . . .

      d. . . . "*OR,* interfering with, obstructing or injuring any lawful business or occupation."

         (1) Specific intent:

(2) Examples:

2. Constitutional conflict:

   a. First Amendment interests:

   b. Effect on private property:

   c. Right to establish regulations:
     A property owner may establish reasonable rules of deportment if they are rationally related to the services performed and the facilities provided.

     (1) Examples:

F. Emergency service act (Govt. Code 8550 to 8668):

1. Introduction:

2. Definition of "emergency":

   A _____, insurrection, unlawful assembly, _____ _____

   or _____ to the laws of the _____ or _____ which

   requires additional _____, _____ or _____ to control.

3. Authority to declare an emergency:

   a. Local emergency:

   b. Statewide or regional emergency:

4. Affect of declaring emergency:

    a. Police power:

    b. Constitutional rights:

        (1) Examples:

    c. National Guard (830.2(c) PC and 143, 146 Mil. and Vet. Code):

Reading Assignment

1. California Penal Code Sections: 69, 148, 151, 171f, 302, 375, 403, 404, 404.6, 405a, 406, 407, 408, 409, 410, 415, 415.5, 416, 417, 596 to 599e, 600, 602.5, 602.10, 602(j), 602(p), 626.2 to 626.9, 647(f), 647(g), 647(c), 647c, 653m, 653q, 723, 726, 727, 4550.

Government Code Sections 8550 to 8668.

Definitions

Define and/or explain the following:

A. Civil protective custody for drunkenness:

B. Disturbing the peace:

C. First Amendment rights:

D. Riot:

E. Rout:

F. Inciting to riot:

G. Rescue:

H. Unlawful assembly:

I. Lynching:

J. Emergency Services Act:

Problem Questions

1. Which statutes described in this chapter require a notice or warning to leave before arrests can be made?

2. Which statutes described in this chapter require at least two participants in order for a violation to occur?

3. You are the community relation's sergeant of your police agency. A teenage group tells you that they plan to conduct a demonstration in front of a bank. The bank is located in a large shopping mall and the entrance is in the roofed-over inside portion of the mall. The entire mall is privately owned property. The bank manager and mall owners object to the demonstration. What advice and warnings do you give to all parties? Include a brief, simple description of the things each party can and cannot do and an explanation of the Penal Code sections involved.

4. What are the treatment procedures that may be used in place of arresting drunks?

5. What are the types of acts that are prohibited under the law of "Disturbing the Peace"?

Chapter 21

Statutes Affecting Juveniles;
Public Health, Safety and Welfare;
And Private Property Rights

Introduction

Although the title of this chapter tries to be specific, it is really the miscellaneous chapter for this book. It includes a variety of laws which affect the safety and well being of both individuals and the public at large. Sections have been devoted to liquor laws, vict laws, drugs and juvenile law. Some are examined in detail in other courses so the material in this chapter has been limited to just a brief introduction to the subjects.

This chapter also examines some statutes relating to trespassing and damage to property. Chapter 20 dealt with similar laws but examined them as they apply to demonstrations and mass disturbances. Some of these laws could have been placed in either chapter but here we will study the statutes designed to control minor trespasses and simple interferences with property rights. Also included in this chapter are laws relating to the ownership and use of firearms.

This then, is the "Miscellaneous" chapter of this book

Objectives

Upon completion of this chapter, you should be able to do the following:

1. Briefly explain the elements of the crimes relating to police authority to close a disaster area.
2. Name at least three other laws relating to the safety of individuals.
3. Define a "public nuisance" and describe the abatement procedures used in such cases.
4. Briefly describe at least four of the common statutes relating to the sale and use of alcoholic beverages.
5. Fully explain the differences between misdemeanor and felony drunk driving; distinguish the terms "drunk" and "under the influence"; and explain the significance of the "implied consent law" and the "presumption of alcoholic influence law."
6. Briefly explain the primary objectives of the federal drug laws and the drug sections of the following California codes: Penal Code, Business and Professions Code, Health and Safety Code, Welfare and Institutions Code.
7. Briefly describe the provisions of the failure to provide laws found in the California Penal Code.
8. List at least four other laws designed to protect the health and safety of juveniles.

9. Explain the maximum and minimum age limits under which a child may fall under the jurisdiction of the juvenile court and the conditions under which he may be transferred to the adult court

10. Describe the conditions under which a child may be made a ward of the juvenile court and explain the basic laws pertaining to police detention of juveniles.

11. Explain the basic format used in most trespass laws and be able to apply it to the description of any of the trespassing laws found in the Penal Code.

12. Define vandalism and describe at least six California laws relating to the damage or destruction of property.

13. Describe the meaning and objectives of "vice" laws.

14. Describe the crimes of prostitution, pimping and pandering.

15. Describe the California obscenity laws.

16. Briefly describe the California prohibitions on gambling.

17. Define "lottery," "endless chain scheme" and "bookmaking."

18. Describe the California laws pertaining to ownership and use of firearms and other weapons.

Lecture Notes Outline

I. Laws affecting public health, safety and welfare:

   A. Laws relating to safety:

   1. Introduction:*There are several types of safety laws. Many are local laws such as city and county building and safety codes.*

   2. Closing disaster areas (409.5 PC):

      a. Authority to close: *The police, sheriff, CHP or Health Officer may close the area around any disaster and the area around the command post.*

      b. Violation:

      Entering and remaining in such area after <u>*being given notice to leave.*</u> *(Must prove that notice had been given.)*

      c. Exception: *News reporters are exempt. However they may be excluded from specific areas, may not interfere with official activities and are responsible for their own safety.*

   3. Impeding police or firefighters at a disaster (402 PC):

      <u>*Stopping*</u> at the scene of a disaster for the purpose of <u>*viewing activities*</u>

      and thereby <u>*impeding*</u> rescue activities. *(Does not prevent someone from stopping to give assistance until the arrival of the police.)*

21-2

4. Leaving a *child* or *handicapped* person in *a locked* *vehicle* . (22156 VC):

5. Making *false report* of an *emergency* (148.3 PC):

B. Laws relating to health and welfare:

1. Public nuisances:

a. Defines (370 PC):

Anything injurious to the health, or *indecent* or *offensive*

to the *senses* , so

as to interfere with the comfortable enjoyment of life or property by *the community.*

(1) Examples: *Prostitution, noxious odors, garbage or trash on property, loud noises from manufacturing in a residential area.*
A nuisance must affect a substantial number of people, not just one person.

b. Enforcement:

(1) 372 PC: *It is a misd. to maintain a public nuisance and refuse to correct it after being given notification.*

(2) Abatement proceedings (373a PC): *It is a misd. for each day that a nuisance continues after being given a notice to correct.*

(a) Duty of district attorney: *The section requires the DA to take some action (very few sections are so worded).*

c. Abatement of other forms of nuisances:

(1) Liquor serving establishments (11200 – 11207 PC): *Prohibits unlawfully selling or giving away liquor.*

(2) House of prostitution or gambling (11225 – 11235 PC): *Applies abatement laws to establishments conducting prostitution or gambling activities.*

(3) Forfeiture provisions (11230PC): *The court may remove and sell all fixture and contents of a public nuisance and may order the premises closed for any use, even by the owner, for one year.*

2. Littering violations:

    a. Definitions of litter and waste material (374 PC): *Any used, discarded or leftover matter (includes garbage, trash, paper, dead animals, cigarette butts, etc).*

    b. Violations:

    (1) Dumping on ___*public*___ or on ___*private*___

    ___*property*___ (374 PC): *(includes roads, highways, public land, parks, and private property if without the owner's consent)*

    (2) Littering any body of water or ___*beaches*___ (374e PC):

    c. Work penalty (374b and 374e PC): *Convicted offended may be given a sentence to work a specified period of time in cleaning us debris from highways, etc.*

3. Spitting in public (372a PC): (Repealed by Statutes 1984)

4. Liquor law violations:

    Note: The following list of liquor law violations is intended to provide just a brief reference guide to this area of the law. A detailed coverage of liquor laws is provided in the courses on juvenile laws and vice investigation.

    a. 25602 B and P code – selling or ___*giving*___ any alcoholic beverage to

    a person who is ___*obviously*___ ___*drunk*___ .

    b. 25631 B and P and 398 PC – sale of alcoholic beverage prohibited between

    ___*2:00*___ A.M. and ___*6:00*___ A.M.

c. 25658 B and P – selling or _____*giving*_____ any alcoholic beverage to a

person under _____*21*_____ or _____*purchase*_____ for such a person.

d. 25662 B and P – any person under 21 having alcoholic beverage in his possession on

_____*any street*_____ or in any place _____*open to the public.*_____

e. 25661 B and P – any person under 21 presenting _____*false identification*_____

for the purpose of _____*buying or obtaining*_____ alcoholic beverages.

f. 25665 B and P – any person under 21 entering premises licensed solely for liquor sales.

C. Driving Under the Influence (23152 and 23153 VC):

1. "Drunk" vs. "Under the Influence": *Drunk – unable to care for safety of self or others Under the influence – Any degree of intoxication that impairs a person's physical or mental abilities.*

2. Presumption of alcoholic influence:

   a. Burden of proof: *The prosecution must prove that the person was under the influence. The defense may present evidence to rebut a presumption of alcoholic influence.*

   b. Presumptions:

      (1) Over .08% blood/alcohol level: *Legal presumption of being under the influence*

      (2) Under .05% blood/alcohol level: *Legal presumption of sobriety.*

      (3) For commercial operators: *Legal presumption of being under the influence* (truck drivers, etc.) *with a blood/alcohol level of over .04%*

      (4) Vessel operators: *All presumption laws apply to all vessel operators also.*

   c. License seizure: *Officers may seize a license on the spot from anyone registering of Blood/alcohol level of over .10%*

3. Implied consent law (**23612**VC): *Any person driving on a public roadway agrees to submit to a test of their blood, urine or breath to determine their blood/alcohol level. A refusal to submit to a test brings a 1 yr. suspension of their license regardless of the outcome of the DUI case.*

4. Driving Under the Influence (Misdemeanor) (23152 VC):

   a. Elements:

      (1) Driving . . .

      (2) . . . while under the influence . . .

      (3) . . . of intoxicating liquor . . .

      (4) . . . or liquor and other drug . . .

   b. Misdemeanor Driving Under the Influence Penalties:

      (1) Very complex penalties with many variations of sentences, based on number of prior convictions and, if the judge chooses to grant probation, mandatory requirements which must be incorporated into the probation conditions.

      Penalties may include:

      (a) Fines of $ *390* to $ *1,000*

      (b) Imprisonment:

         (from *two* days to *four* years possible)
         (optional felony on 4th conviction)

      (c) License restriction up to *120* days.
          (may drive to work only)

      (d) License suspension up to *30* months.
          (license reinstated w/o testing)

      (e) License revocation up to *4* years.
          (must take test for new license)

      (f) Successful completion of alcohol rehabilitation program. *All convicted offenders are required to attend, and successfully complete, an alcohol education and rehabilitation program.*

5. Driving Under the Influence (Felony) (23153 VC):

    a. Elements:

        (1) Driving . . .

        (2) . . . while under the influence . . .

        (3) . . . of intoxicating liquor . . .

        (4) . . . or liquor and other drug . . .

        AND . . .

        (5) __*violating*__ any law . . .

        (6) which causes __*injury*__

          to anyone other than __*himself*__

    b. Felony Driving Under the Influence penalties:

        (1) Fines of $ __*390*__ to $ __*1,000*__

        (2) Imprisonment:

          From __*90*__ days to __*4*__ years.

        (3) License suspension up to __12__ months.
          (license reinstated w/o testing)

        (4) License revocation up to __*3*__ years.
          (must take test for new license)

        (5) Successful completion of alcohol rehabilitation program. *Required of all convicted offenders.*

D. Crimes related to driving under the influence:

    1. Drinking in __*a motor vehicle*__ (23221 VC):

    2. Possession of __*open container*__
       in a motor vehicle (23222 VC):

    3. Drinking while driving (23220 VC): *Used when a driver is drinking but not DUI*

E. Drug laws:

    1. Introduction: *There are a wide variety of laws controlling illegal drug use. Theses laws are characterized by constant change in the statutes and judicial interpretation. Enforcement and prosecution policies will vary also.*

21-7

2. Comparison of state and federal drug laws: *While the laws will often overlap federal enforcement attempts to control the manufacture, importation, large wholesalers, interstate and international drug activities. State enforcement concentrates on local distribution and individual use.*

3. California statutes relating to drug abuse:

   a. Penal Code:

      (1) Bringing drugs into or using drugs in ___*jails*___ or ___*prisons.*___ (4573 – 4573.6 PC):

      (2) ___*False impersonation as a doctor*___ in order to obtain drugs (377 PC):

      (3) ___*Inhaling fumes*___ of ___*glue*___ *(toluene)*
          and other volatile substances (381 PC):

   b. Business and Professions Code:

      (1) Controls possession, sale and use of ___*hypodermic needles*___
          (4140 – 4164 B and P):

      (2) Control of ___*poisons*___ (4160 – 4164 B and P):

      (3) Control of ___*dangerous drugs*___ including ___*barbiturates*___

          and ___*amphetamines*___ (4211 – 4390.5 B and P):

   c. Welfare and Institutions Code:

      (1) Administration of ___*narcotic rehabilitation programs*___ (3000 – 3201 WIC):

   d. Health and Safety Code:

      (1) Establishes California Controlled Substances Act (11000 – 11651 H and S):

      (2) Establishes classifications of drugs: Over ___*120*___ drugs in

          ___*five*___ classes (11053 – 11058 H and S Code).

      Includes:

          Opium
          Heroin
          Morphine
          Codeine
          Cocaine
          LSD
          Marijuana
          Peyote
          THC
          Mescaline
          Psilocybin   Etc.

21-8

(3) Defines criminal acts in relation to above drugs.

Sections 11377 through 11382 H & S

(4) Prescribes penalties for violations (11350 – 11363 H and S):

Penalties vary from small fines to 7 years in prison.

(5) Controls manufacture, sales, distribution and prescriptions for drugs:

11379.6 H & S

(6) Marijuana (11357 – 11631 H and S):

Covers possession, cultivation, sales, transportation, etc. of marijuana.

(7) Drug paraphernalia (11364 – 11364.7 and 11014.5 H and S):

Covers manufacturing, sales, possession, etc. of opium pipes and other drug paraphernalia.

e. Variables affecting drug penalties:

(1) Type of drug:

Most serious Heroin, etc. – Least serious Marijuana.

(2) Number of prior convictions:

Prior convictions can increase the severity of the penalty.

(3) Activity with drugs:

(a) *Simple possession for personal use.*

(b) *Possession for sales.*

(c) *Actual sales.*

(d) *Sales to a minor.*

f. Enforcement, prosecution and sentencing philosophies:

The emphasis will shift depending on the particular drug problems at the time.

II. Vice laws:

    A. Introduction:

        1. "Vice" defined:

        Activities that conflict with the moral, ethical or religious beliefs of the majority of the society.

        2. Overview of section:

            a. *Prostitution*

            b. *Obscenity and pornography*

            c. *Gambling*

        3. Objectives of vice laws:

        To protect the integrity of structure of families and to prevent social decay. (All of history's great civilizations – Egyptians, Greeks, Romans, etc. collapsed from within.)

    B. Prostitution offenses:

        1. Prostitution (**647(b)** PC):

        (Part of *disorderly conduct* statute.)

            a. *Soliciting* or *engaging* in lewd act . . .

                (1) Type of act: *Must be an overt act, not just vulgar conversation, but not necessarily intercourse (Hugh Grant & Miss Devine).*

                (2) Completion of act: *The crime is completed upon solicitation with a serious intent.*

            b. . . . between persons . . .
            Both the prostitute and the customer are guilty.

                (1) Sex of parties: *The sex of the parties is immaterial.*

                (2) Status of parties: *It does not matter who was the prostitute and who was the customer.*

            c. . . . for *money* or *other valuable consideration.* *(Consensual sex between adults is a crime only if it is paid for.)*

2. Pimping (266 PC):

   a. Deriving ___*support*___ , in whole or ___*in part*___ ,
      from the earnings of a prostitute . . .

   OR

   ___*Soliciting*___ for a prostitute. *(Engaging customers or managing the activities of a prostitute(s).)*

3. Pandering (266i PC):

   a. ___*Procuring*___ a prostitute for another,
      (Frequently involves hotel clerks, bell hops, cab drivers or bartenders)

   OR

   b. ___*Persuading*___ or ___*encouraging*___ another to become a prostitute.

4. Penalties:

   Prostitute: *Min. 45 days – Max. 90 days (unless there are prior convictions.)*

   Pimp: *3, 4 or 6 years*

   Panderer: *3, 4 or 6 years*

C. Obscenity offenses (311 – 313.5 PC):

   1. "Obscene"

      Matter that to the average person, applying contemporary statewide standards, appeals to the prurient interest, that, taken as a whole, depicts or describes sexual conduct in a patently offensive way, and that, taken as a whole, lacks serious literary, artistic, political or scientific value.

   2. Harmful matter: *Includes printed or written material, drawings, photos, movies, statutes, recordings or electronic transmissions.*

   3. Current status: *Communities cannot determine what is acceptable or not based on local standards. Generally, while live sex acts in public or any place open to the public can be prohibited, most other nude performances have found protection under the 1st Amendment.*

D. Gambling offenses:

    1. Lotteries (319 – 326 PC): *Any scheme for the distribution of property by chance among persons who have paid a valuable consideration (raffles, football pools, etc.)*

    2. Endless chains (327 PC): *Any scheme to acquire property by enlisting greater and greater numbers of people, each of whom contributes to the originators (pyramids, etc).*

    3. Gaming (330 PC): *Prohibits dice, cards, roulette or any other game where the "house" takes a percentage of the winnings or collects a profit margin on wins and losses in a game.*

        a. "Poker and Bingo Parlors" (326.5 and 337s PC): *Local cities may license non-profit Bingo operators and certain forms of poker and other types of games if approved by the voters.*

    4. Slot machines (330a – 337 PC): *Prohibits the manufacture, sales or possession of any slot machine.*

        a. Exceptions:

            (1) Games of skill (330.5 PC): *Games of skill, pinball, amusement machine, etc. are exempted.*

            (2) Aboard vessels (330.6 PC): *Slot machines aboard cruise ships are exempted but cannot be used while within the 3-mile limit.*

    5. Bookmaking (337a PC): *Off track betting on horse races is prohibited except at para-mutual locations. All other types of race or sports betting are prohibited*

    6. Fraudulent Carnival Games (334 PC): *Prohibits carnival games that are rigged so as to reduce a patron's chances of winning.*

E. Laws relating to the safety and welfare of juveniles and other special populations:

Note: The following section on juvenile law is intended to provide just a brief introduction to this area of law. A detailed coverage of most of these laws is provided in courses on juvenile procedures.

    1. Failure to provide laws:

        a. Introduction: *Several sections of the law require the financial or other types of support of one group by another.*

b. Statutes:

    (1) Child support (270 PC):

        (a) Requires __*parent*__ of either __*legitimate*__ or

        __*illegitimate*__ child to provide support of a child.

    (2) Support of spouse (270a PC): *Requires a husband or wife to provide for the support of a spouse who is unable to care for themselves.*

    (3) Support of indigent parent (270c PC): *Requires adult children to support an indigent parent. (If not done the child must repay Welfare for support of the parent.)*

2. Laws protecting the safety and health of juveniles:

    a. Child abandonment (271 PC): *Desertion of a child under 14 with the intent to abandon by the parent or other person having responsibility for the child.*

    b. 653 PC - __*Tattooing*__ a minor under 18 years.

    c. 308 PC – selling or giving __*tobacco*__ to minors under age of 18:

        (1) Does not prohibit __*possession*__ or __*smoking*__ by the minor:

        (2) Exception (308a PC): *Repealed by statutes, 1989*

3. Laws protecting morals of juveniles:

    a. Immoral practices in presence of children (273g PC): *Prohibits habitual drunkenness, prostitution, sexual activity, drug use, etc. in the presence of children.*

    b. Contributing to the delinquency of a minor (272 PC): *Prohibits any activity that is likely to adversely influence a child under 18 (e.g. causing or encouraging sex acts, drinking, truancy, runaway, etc).*

4. Juvenile court laws (300 – 914 Welfare and Institutions Code):

    a. Jurisdiction of juvenile court:

        (1) Minimum age for juvenile court: *None*

        (2) Minimum age for CYA commitment (733 WIC): *8 years old.*

        (3) Minimum age for adult court and state prison commitment (603, 707 WIC): *14 years old*

(4) Maximum age for juvenile court (607 WIC): *Normally 21 – 25 under certain circumstances.*

(5) Maximum age for CYA commitment (607 WIC): *Up to age 25 depending on the crime that resulted in the commitment.*

b. Conditions under which a juvenile may be made a ward of the court:

(1) Dependent child (300 WIC): *Dependent, abused, abandoned or neglected child.*

(2) Habitually disobedient or truant (601 WIC): *Status offenses.*

(3) Delinquent child (602 WIC): *Juvenile who commits an act that would be a crime if committed by an adult.*

c. Detention procedures:

(1) Police may detain if (305, 625 WIC):

(a) *Probable cause to believe that 300 WIC applies.*

(b) *Probable cause to believe that the juvenile has committed a 602 WIC offense.*

(c) *Any child in need of immediate medical care.*

(2) Procedure after detention (307 – 309, 626 – 629 WIC):

(a) Release to parents or   *deliver to juvenile hall.*

(b) Notice to parents: *The parent(s) or guardian (s) must be immediately notified of the juvenile's detention.*

(c) Telephone calls: *A juvenile is entitled to 2 calls, one to a parent or guardian, the other to an employer or attorney.*

(d) Advising of rights: *The juvenile must be advised of his/her rights immediately after arrest whether s/he is to be questioned or not.*

d. Court procedures: *A juvenile has all the rights that an adult has except for a right to bail or jury trial. The same rules of evidence, etc. apply.*

II. Laws affecting property rights:

   A. Trespassing:

      1. Introduction: *There are many different trespassing statutes, each with differing requirements. None are serious enough to permit the use of deadly force (contrary to what some homeowners believe).*

      2. Common format of trespass statutes:

         a. Type of act prohibited: *Range from mere loitering on or near property to actually taking up total occupancy.*

         b. Type of property involved: *Some sections apply only to dwellings while others to any type of structure while still other sections apply to buildings, land or any other location.*

         c. Type of enclosure or posting required: *Some sections require no posting or fencing while others are very specific (e.g. signs with specific wording every 600' apart).*

         d. Special additional elements: *Some sections require that the entry be made for a specific purpose (e.g. hunting, to damage property, etc).*

Note: The chart on the following page lists all of the major statutes relating to trespassing. It is arranged according to the common format for trespass statutes as described above.

The chart has been deliberately left incomplete in order to allow you to familiarize yourself with these laws by examining the code sections.

ASSIGNMENT: Locate each code section listed on the chart. Read the section in the Penal Code and then fill in the blank spaces left in the chart.

Penal Code Section	Type of Prohibited Activities	Enclosure or Posting Required	Type of Property Affected	Special Additional Elements
647(g)	Loitering, Prowling or wandering	None required	Any private Property business	(1) At nighttime only (2) Without lawful business
647(h)	Same	Same	Same	*Same plus peeking in door or window of inhabited bldg*
647(i)	*Lodging (sleeping)*	Same	Any building or Other place	Without consent of owner
602(h)	*Willfully opening or damaging any fence*	Must be fenced	Any enclosed land	None
602(i)	*Building fires*	*No trespass signs every mile*	Any lands	Without consent of Owner
602(j)	*Entering*	None required	Any lands	For the purpose of injuring property or interfering with the owner's business
602(k)	Same	Posting not required if cultivated or enclosed	Any cultivated, enclosed or posted land	*Requires posting (3 pre mile & at entrances) if not cultivated.*
602(l)	*Entering and occupying*	None required	Any structure	Without consent of owner
602(m)	*Driving a veh.*	Same	Any land	Same
602(n)	Refusing to leave	Same	Any land or structure	Upon request of owner or police
602.5	Entering or remaining	None required	*Any dwelling*	Without consent of owner
603	Forcibly entering	None required	*Any dwelling or cabin*	Damages, injures or destroys any property
552 to 555.5	Entering, remaining on or loitering near	Very specific posting requirements	Certain specified industrial property	None

B. Vandalism and destruction of property:

1. General vandalism section (594PC):

   a. Definition: *Any deliberate damage to or destruction to the property of another. (One spouse may vandalize the community property of the other – Jim Brown.)*

   b. Penalties:

      (1) Under $1,000 damage: *Max 6 months.*

      (2) $1,000 - $5,000 damage: *Max. 1 year.*

      (3) Over $5,000 damage: *16 months, 2 or 3 years.*

2. Defacing property with paint (594.5 PC): *Allows cities and counties to regulated the sales of spray paint.*

3. Other penal code sections relating to property damage or destruction:

587 and 587a	Railroad care, tracks and railroad facilities:
588	Digging up or flooding highways:
588a	Throwing glass or other substances on highway:
588b	Road signs, barriers and warning lights:
590	Highway mileage signs:
591	Telephone and telegraph lines:
592	Irrigation canals, gates, flumes and ditches:
593	Electrical power lines and equipment:
593c	Gas lines and mains:
602a and b	Wood and timber:
602c	Produce:
602d and e	Earth, soil and rock
602f	Road signs:
602g	Oyster and shellfish beds:
602h	Fences and "no shooting" signs:

604	Standing crops:
605	Survey landmarks:
606	Jail buildings and cells:
607	Dams, levees, canals and bridges:
622	Monuments and shade trees:
622 ½	Objects or places of historical interest:
624	Water pipe lines:

C. Repossession of property: *This is usually a civil matter where a purchaser has failed to make payments and the finance company recovers the property. The role of the officer is to keep the peace, not to try an interpret the contract.*

D. Landlord/Tenant disputes: *This is usually a civil matter where again the role of the officer is to keep the peace. Landlord/Tenant disputes are covered in detail in the Concepts of Enforcement Services course.*

III. Weapons Laws:

A. Federal Law: *Most federal law deals with the interstate sales, foreign importation and exportation of weapons and ammunition and the possession of certain types of weapons (military, machine guns, etc.). Federal law is enforced by the Bureau of Alcohol, Tobacco and Firearms.*

B. California State Law (12000 – 12654 PC):

1. General: *California firearms laws are found in the Penal Code (Sections 12000 through12550. Firearms laws are also found in the Vehicle Code, Fish and Came Code, Welfare and Institutions Code and the Business and Professions Code.*

2. Firearms Sales and Registration: *Any person who engages in the advertising, selling or transferring of firearms must be licensed.*

A private party selling a firearm to another private party must complete the transaction through a dealer.

Firearms dealers must keep a record of all transactions, including a complete description of the firearm and the purchaser.

a. Ex-Felons: *All persons convicted of a felony are prohibited from owning or possessing any firearm.*

3. Age Restrictions:

   a. Firearms and ammunitions sales: *It is a misdemeanor to sell or furnish any firearm, air gun, gas-operated gun or spring operated BB gung, designed to fire a metal projectile, to any person under 18.*

   b. Firearms and ammunition possession: *A person under 18 may not possess any firearm or ammunition except under the direct supervision of a parent, guardian or responsible adult.*

4. Possession and use of concealable weapons:

   a. Definitions and included weapons: *A concealable firearm is any weapon having a barrel less than 12" that is designed to expel a projectile.*

   b. Restrictions: *It is a felony for any alien, drug addict or anyone convicted of a felony to own or possess a concealable firearm*
   It is illegal to sell or give a concealable firearm to a person reasonable y believed to be an ex-felon, alien, drug addict or person under 18.
   It is illegal to carry a concealable firearm on the person or in a vehicle if the firearm is concealed. (Firearms in a vehicle must be unloaded, in a carrying case and locked in the trunk, if no trunk the case must be locked.)

   c. Exceptions: *Any citizen over 18 (except those prohibited by Sec. 12021) may possess a concealable firearm in his home or place of business and no permit or license to purchase, own, possess or keep any such firearm is required.*

      Peace officers and other persons exempted are listed in Sec. 12027 PC.

5. Possession and use of other weapons:

6. Other weapons laws:

Reading Assignment:

1. California Penal Code:

   148.3, 266(h) and (i), 270, 270a – 270c, 271, 272, 273a, 273d, 273g, 308, 308a, 311 – 315.5, 319 – 337a, 346, 370 – 374c, 377, 381, 384g, 398, 401, 402, 402b – 402d, 409.5, 552 – 555.5, 587 – 594, 594.5, 602(a) – 602(p), 602.5, 603 – 607, 647(b), 622 – 624, 647(g), (h) and (i), 653, 4573 – 4573.6, 11200 – 11207, 11225 – 11318, 12000 – 12654.

2. Business and Professions Code:

   4140 – 4164, 4211 – 4390.5, 25602, 25631, 25658, 25661, 25662, 25665.

3. Welfare and Institutions Code:

   300, 305, 307 – 309, 600, 601, 602, 603, 607, 625, 625.1, 626, 627, 627.5, 707, 733, 3000 – 3201.

4. Health and Safety Code:

   11000 – 11651.

5. Vehicle Code:

   22156, 23152, 23153, 23220 – 23223.

Definitions

Define or explain the following terms:

A. Public nuisance: *Anything injurious to the health, or indecent or offensive to the senses so as to interfere with the comfortable enjoyment of life or property by the community.*

B. Abatement proceeding: *The D.A. must take some action. It is a misd. for each day that a nuisance continues after notice has been given.*

C. Under the influence: *Any degree of intoxication that impairs a person's physical or mental abilities.*

D. Implied consent law: *Any person driving a motor vehicle agrees to submit to a blood/alcohol test of their blood, breath or urine.*

E. Indigent: *A person without financial means of support or insufficient financial means.*

F. Dependent child: *Any person under 18 falling within one of the descriptions of Sec. 300 WIC.*

G. Delinquent child: *Any person under 18 who commits an act a described by Sec. 602 WIC.*

H. Ticket scalping: *Resale of an admission ticket on the premises of where the event is to be held.*

I. Malicious mischief: *Maliciously defacing, damaging or destroying the personal or real property of another.*

J. Legal presumption of alcoholic influence: *A blood/alcohol level or .08 or higher.*

K. Vice: *Activities that conflict with the moral, ethical or religious beliefs of the majority of the society.*

L. Prostitution: *Soliciting or engaging in lewd acts between persons in exchange for money or other valuable considerations.*

M. Pimping: *Deriving support in whole or in part from the earnings of a prostitute or soliciting for a prostitute.*

N. Pandering: *Procuring a prostitute for another or persuading or encouraging another to become a prostitute.*

O. Obscene: *Matter, taken as a whole, that to the average person, applying contemporary statewide standards, appeals to the prurient interest, that, taken as a whole, depicts or describes sexual conduct in a patently offensive way, and that, taken as a whole, lacks serious literary, artistic, political or scientific value.*

P. Lottery: *Any scheme for the distribution of property by chance among persons who have paid a valuable consideration.*

Q. Endless chain: *Any scheme to acquire property by enlisting greater and greater numbers of people, each of whom contributes to the originators.*

R. Gaming: *Dice, cards, roulette or any other game where the house takes a percentage of the winnings or collects a profit margin on the wins and losses in a game.*

S. Bookmaking: *Accepting of track bets on horse races or on any other type of race or sporting event.*